Parents at Last

Parents at Last

Celebrating Adoption and the New Pathways to Parenthood

CYNTHIA V. N. PECK AND WENDY WILKINSON

Photographs by Helen Kolikow Garber

CLARKSON POTTER/PUBLISHERS
NEW YORK

In loving memory of my father whose passing was the catalyst that brought Alexandra Willa into our lives. And to my mother, sister, and husband who knew I was meant to be a mother.
W.W.

To my children, Benjamin, Emilie-elisabeth, Caroline, Christopher, Alison, Meredith, and Abigail. Being your mom has defined my life and has been my greatest reward.
C.V.N.P.

Copyright © 1998 by Cynthia Peck and Wendy Wilkinson

Photographs © 1998 by Helen K. Garber; Additional photographs supplied by John Ehrendou (p. 114), Joan Kingdon (p. 133), Charlie Knoeckel (p. 153), Phil Long (p. 75), and Evelyne McNamara (p. 46).

Published by Clarkson N. Potter/Publishers, 201 East 50th Street, New York, New York 10022. Member of the Crown Publishing Group.

Random House, Inc. New York, Toronto, London, Sydney, Auckland

www.randomhouse.com

CLARKSON N. POTTER, POTTER, and colophon are trademarks of Clarkson N. Potter, Inc.

Printed in the United States of America

Design by Maggie Hinders

Library of Congress Cataloging-in-Publication Data

Peck, Cynthia

Parents at last: celebrating adoption and the new pathways to parenthood / Cynthia Peck and Wendy Wilkinson.

1. Adoption. 2. Parenthood. 3. Parenting—Psychological aspects.

4. Family. I. Wilkinson, Wendy. II. Title.

HV875.P384 1998

362.73'4—dc21

98-15737

CIP

ISBN 0-609-60290-X

10 9 8 7 6 5 4 3 2 1

First Edition

Acknowledgments

WE ARE GRATEFUL to the families who opened their lives in order to share their experience, hope, and joy on the path to parenthood. Their flexibility, honesty, and patience with the process—through rewriting, rescheduling, revising, reshooting—is no less than they show to their own families. Thanks!

We also extend our appreciation to our agents, Selene Ahn, Alex Smithline, and David Vigliano, who encouraged our work as a team, and to our editor, Pam Krauss, for her faith in us and her support as we took our first baby steps through the process.

Thanks also to Stuart Garber who put his medical career on hold to assist in photographing the families and AGFA for providing the film and processing.

Finally, to our own families, who ate late, rose early, rearranged their own schedules to accommodate ours, and who, along with our closest friends, listened to each of us go on for hours on end, a *special* thanks. You are our heroes, the true "stuff" of family!

Contents

Introduction

From Cindy . . .

WHEN I WAS THIRTY-SOMETHING AND SINGLE back in the early seventies and realized that adoption was probably going to be the only way I'd ever have the family I had dreamed of all my life, I didn't know where to turn. I couldn't pick up a magazine and read personal success stories about adoption, and the Internet did not yet exist. In fact, back then I didn't even know anyone who was adopted or who *had* adopted. As a teacher in the public school system, I occasionally heard whispers among my colleagues about some child or another in one of our classes whose academic or behavioral problems were probably because (had I heard?) he was *adopted*. In many circles, the stigma of adoption was as shameful as any scarlet *A* ever worn. But I wanted someone to call me "mom," and I would have given my eyeteeth to have been able to sit down and have a heart-to-heart talk with *anyone* who could have given me some hope and direction.

How my life has changed since then! For two and a half decades, adoption and parenthood have defined my life and been my most rewarding journey. I have adopted seven children and raised nine. Six are newly independent, self-supporting, college-educated, career-minded young adults. Three are still in high school and are looking forward with nervous excitement to the choices they must soon make.

I never saw myself as a pioneer when I decided to adopt as a single parent. When something feels right I trust my instinct, knowing that things have a way of working out for the best. Imagine my surprise when I learned sometime after the arrival of my second child in 1979 that there were fewer than one hundred agency-based adoptions by

single parents in this country. Reading this staggering statistic in the *New York Times,* I wondered if I'd been counted twice. Things have certainly changed.

My income from teaching supported us, and we all supported one another in the growing years. We tried to approach each day with a feeling of abundance rather than a sense of deprivation. We lived in an affluent area, where it would have been easy to look at life as a glass half empty, but I tried hard to point out to my family that that sort of thinking was a choice and probably not a very good way to approach things. I remember a discussion we had around the dinner table one night on that very topic. The general consensus was that although many of my kids' friends had a good deal more than they did in terms of material things, there were also many who had less. I remember Emilie adding, "but none of them knows how to be as responsible as we are, Mom. We're tops at that!" She was right; they certainly were.

Consider this, for example. In complete secrecy, my kids threw a surprise (yes, I really *was* surprised) fiftieth birthday party for me five years ago. They had been planning it for over a year, right down to the engraved invitations (and I thought I knew everything that went on at home). In the four hours that Alison, Abby, and I were out of the house attending Meredith's dance recital, the remaining six transformed our backyard for the celebration. They set up an enormous wedding tent, fifteen tables, 140 chairs, and badminton, volleyball, and basketball courts. They orchestrated a cocktail hour and a five-course, sit-down dinner for over a hundred guests—all of whom were already in place and waiting patiently for me, the guest of honor, to come home. Ben, then a high school senior and my first child, gave a champagne toast. I cried, and everyone cheered.

We have shared love, secrets, advice, pain, and prayers in our journey as a family. And although in many ways it's been harder than I ever imagined it could be, the rewards have also been greater than I ever dreamed. Was it worth it? Yes—every single step, every single minute. Ups and downs, laughter and tears. Together we've opened doors I never knew existed. We've done it all.

From Wendy . . .

L IKE EVERY OTHER MAJOR, LIFE-CHANGING CHOICE I've made in life, the decision to have a child was not an easy one to make. I did not get married until my late thirties, and I had never felt a burning desire to get pregnant. Actually, the joke between me and my husband, Dennis, was that if I happened to become pregnant, *he* would have to carry the child for the last trimester. But, truthfully, I never felt that I had to have that biological connection to be a good mother.

I thrived on a wild and very busy career path for almost two decades, and somehow I never had the inclination, opportunity, or time to have children. I started my own tiny public relations and marketing company, literally on my dining room table, and *it* was my "baby." But by the time I turned forty, I began to evaluate my life a bit more deeply. Although I still loved to travel, the other "perks" of my career, such as eating at fabulous restaurants, shopping, and indulging in stress-busting massages, were not as important to me as they once had been. The plight of the thousands of children warehoused in Romania was a big news story at the time, and Dennis and I were drawn to the heart-wrenching images of those precious babies abandoned in grim orphanages in a country in turmoil. We mentioned the word *adoption* to each other more than once, but before we knew it another year had gone flying by.

Then one day my father, who had been completely healthy, suffered a major cardiac aneurysm, and things changed abruptly for me. As our family gathered around his hospital bed, encouraging—almost willing—him to survive his surgery, I realized that I didn't want this love and strong bond to end with Dennis and me.

My father died five weeks later. The next morning I had breakfast with a woman who had adopted her beautiful four-year-old girl, Emily, from Korea when she was four months old. She gave me a tattered copy of the *New York Times* Sunday magazine that featured a story on Chinese adoption. I took one look at that baby's beautiful face and knew that China was where we should go to find our child.

Although we had been ambivalent about becoming parents, Dennis and I nonetheless had talked about favorite names—Alexander for a boy and Alexandra for a girl. Once firm in our decision to adopt from China, Alexandra Willa, in loving memory of my father William, became our focus long before we even had a formal referral with birthdate and photo. Eager to move forward once we made up our minds, we were through the paperwork and on a plane to China seven months later.

Once there, the reality of our decision hit me. With very little preparation, no real identification with Alex's country or culture, and no time to bond, I suddenly had a three-month-old infant placed in my arms. All around us new parents were crying with joy, while I was thinking, "Oh my God! What have I done?" Suffering physically already from possible food poisoning, the flu, or maybe just severe stress, my body and mind rebelled at all I was doing and serious second thoughts entered my mind. Even following our very shaky twenty-four-hour trip back to Los Angeles, I was still not sure if I was ready to be a mother.

After three months of sleepless nights and exhausted days, I was able to work through my fears, and I began to realize how my daughter had added a new dimension to our lives. Alex has brought me more joy, and sometimes greater pain, than I ever knew I could endure. I frequently think about our trip to China and the morning our group of twenty-two met for breakfast the day after receiving our daughters. I remember remarking how amazing it was that those eleven tiny beings could turn a group of middle-aged professionals into baby-talking, proud-as-punch parents.

For me this book has been a work in progress for the last three years. It began when I returned from China and met so many other people who, like Dennis and me, had finally become parents. While researching this book, Cindy and I also found many other wonderful and strong families who deeply felt the need to bring another child or children into their lives to make their family circle complete. Although we had taken many different paths to bring children into our lives, our journeys were in many ways the same. And each of us learned valuable lessons along the way.

*T*HE DESIRE TO BECOME PARENTS HAS NEVER BEEN so visible, antici- pated, or talked about as it is today. It is difficult to pick up a woman's magazine, celebrity newspaper, or newsmagazine and not find a story about proud new parents, a heartwarming adoption, or the heartbreak of insurmountable infertility. Never have there been so many ways to become parents as there are today. Both domestic and inter- national adoptions are dramatically on the rise, and high-tech options, from in vitro fer- tilization to surrogacy are meeting with increased success.

The stories in this collection have been organized into four sections that roughly parallel the stages of growth in families. Part One, "In the Beginning," describes families flush with the excitement of their decision to pursue an alternative approach to parent- hood. We all know of somebody in this situation, whether they are coming to terms with a real sense of loss or feeling pressured by the reality that time may be running out for them. For these people it is parenthood *now*—or possibly *never.*

Part Two, "The Wonder Years," tells the stories of families that have been together a little longer and are settling in to their new roles and responsibilities. The "newness" of their experience is fading, and as their family life widens to include activities such as play groups, preschool, day care, and outings, these parents often have to deal with ques- tions—from their children and from others—about how they came to be a family. And sometimes they confront prejudice. What was once exclusively the parent's story is now the child's story as well. How it shall be shared, and with whom, becomes a concern.

There is a lot going on in the families that contribute their stories to Part Three, "In the Parenting Trenches," which covers the years just before and during adolescence. These resilient parents know when to stand firm and when to bend. They appear com- fortable with the choices they have made and are committed to the growth of all fam- ily members. They know how to play and have fun together, too. Their capacity for optimism, honesty, resourcefulness, and perseverance in the face of daily challenges appears boundless. At the heart of their success is the way they convey their acceptance and understanding to their children while stressing the family's values.

Are you curious about the long-range outcomes of decisions to adopt or create a family with the help of medical technology? Part Four, "Pioneer Wisdom," lets you glimpse the future through stories told by those who have already lived out those decisions. Four adoptive families, their children now grown, talk about their experiences at a time when adoption was a less obvious choice and there was little support available to help them "walk through" the experience. An adult adoptee shares her views on the impact of transracial adoption on lives. Finally, a single mother, the first to be artificially inseminated in her state over twenty years ago, speaks to the strength of her desire to give birth, measured against the prejudice and hostility of her community. Few others have as many years behind them to address this viewpoint from a distance. We think you will find the shared wisdom of these contributors reassuring and thought-provoking.

Without a doubt, the most common solutions to the problem of infertility—adoption and hi-tech medical intervention—are making parenthood possible for more people than ever before. Adoption and infertility issues are "out of the closet" and discussed openly in the media. There are support groups for those grieving from infertility, for others participating in ever-newer fertility treatments, and for those exploring adoption options. Information is available in abundance with the click of a mouse and a quick jump on the Internet. Age, marital status, gender, and lifestyle no longer limit one's opportunity to set out on the pathway to parenthood.

Hearing each new story has enriched our own understanding of the ongoing and continually challenging process of creating a family. We hope we have created a book that will be read and enjoyed by all, whether or not all of our readers are directly connected to adoption or the infertility struggle. We want *Parents at Last* to serve as an inspiration and a guide to those who cannot or chose not to create a family in the traditional way, as well as to the extended families and friends from whom they draw support.

Part I

In the Beginning

· ·

T HE STORIES IN THIS SECTION DEMONSTRATE the sheer determination and almost unbelievable faith and courage of would-be parents as they pursue their dream of creating or adding to their families. Still basking in the afterglow and excitement of new parenthood, these parents have not yet had to confront the problems of race, prejudice, and identity—both cultural and biological—that will inevitably come into play. Friends and strangers alike are still in the "What a darling baby!" mode, and the parents themselves are full of unbridled optimism. Parents at last, none of these families can imagine their lives without these particular children.

This is not to suggest, however, that their pathways to parenthood were without bumps. Several of these families were created in response to an initial loss and a sense of despair. Family members frequently had to adjust to bringing a new and perhaps very different presence into the family circle. And those same family members sometimes went to incredible lengths to help their loved ones create the family that they so desperately desired. For one couple it took the help of a younger sister to make having children a reality. In one remarkable act of faith, a new friend came to the aid of a couple who desperately wanted biological children but could not carry a pregnancy to full term.

Many of these parents were in their forties when they finally completed their families, and one a single career officer, well into his sixties, created his family by traveling halfway around the world to bring his seven-year-old son home from Russia. Two of these couples battled with infertility for years before turning to adoption to fulfill their dream of having a family. As you will see, age, marital status, and sexual orientation are no longer barriers to parenthood.

One notable similarity in each of these family histories is these parents' willingness to pursue alternatives. Most of these families had to accept and then embrace a new idea about how to create their family that was perhaps very different from their original notion. And though they differ in their particulars, each of these stories has the same wonderful outcome. Regardless of the difficulty, heartbreak, and almost insurmountable odds, these parents continued toward their heart's desire until they found their children.

From Infertility to Adoption

JAY AND BROOK S. DOUGHERTY

LOS ANGELES, CALIFORNIA

Shots in the butt
peeing in cups
test that turn blue
cash spent
hospitalized, anesthetized, traumatized
elusive eggs
failed again
abdominal scars—
and no baby

Not all miracle babies are those in the photos that fill the office walls of infertility specialists. Whether initiated in a petri dish or through the miracle of adoption, becoming a parent comes down to being in the right place at the right time. And with adoption, the whole chain of events takes on such mystical proportions that biology hardly seems worth quibbling about.

*J*AY WAS THE FIRST MAN I DATED whom I also could imagine as a daddy. We decided that we'd get married if I got pregnant. I wanted a wedding. I wanted wedding presents. But most of all, I wanted a baby. I was thirty-four. We knew we were meant to be parents. We knew our baby was just waiting to be fertilized—and we were right, our baby *was* waiting to be fertilized, by someone else's sperm in someone else's tummy. No one mentioned that possibility. Now we wish they had, because it is so much more pleasant to search for your baby in a world of humans than in the labyrinths of hospital corridors.

with air, like an old tire. This test is a must if you haven't experienced excruciating pain in that area of your body. It provides all the thrills of labor, but with no baby.

We found out my tubes were both shot. That called for major surgery. Three hours under anesthesia and my tubes were "fixed." Three weeks in bed followed, and six months before I felt completely human again. Meanwhile we had a huge wedding and got lots of presents. "Have regular sex," my gynecologist, Dr. Newman, said. *Regular* is hardly the word that leaps to mind when I think of temperature charts and endearments such as, "We have to do it right this second." Eight months went by—and no baby. When my doctor mentioned adoption, I bit his head off.

It was time to see a specialist. The specialist had lots of pictures of miracle babies on his walls, none of them adopted. Adoption was not considered the miracle that it is. This guy wanted to get a look at my insides. It was time for laparoscopy number one.

We were told that in vitro fertilization was the answer for us—the only answer. Did we want to go to an orientation class at the hospital? Hey, what's eleven thousand dollars when there's a 6 percent chance of success? The hospital orientation staff deemphasized (that is, failed to mention) the fact that the people who succeeded usually spent eleven thousand dollars over and over and over again. Of course, they don't tell you it's eleven thousand

After we had tried for six months to conceive, gynecological shadows from the past suggested that maybe there was a problem. I purchased an ovulation predictor kit. Our lives incorporated my early-morning potty visits. I peed in a cup at 6 A.M. and bungled a test that only had three steps to it. Next came fertility pills, followed by that ever-popular test in which my fallopian tubes were blown up

dollars. They tell you it's six. And then you're billed for the rest, which includes such wonders as the hundred-dollar sanitary napkin. Your insurance is supposed to cover these overages. It rarely does. Infertility is not an illness or a disease. Neither is being a jerk, which is what we felt like when we got the bill.

And still we weren't ready to adopt. First we had to finish trying to find our baby in a petri dish. But not until I took hormones. Lots of hormones. When I went to get my prescription filled, my druggist told me that the last time he had filled a hormone prescription of that strength it was for a guy preparing for a sex-change operation. Jay turned out to be terrific at giving me my daily shots. He played nice music. I bent over. In went the magic, and up went our hopes. We have a poster above our bed of a long line of little babies. We sat below it, and Jay played children's songs on his guitar. We prayed that our baby would hear us and know how to find us. It was a good idea, but we were looking in the wrong place. Days of shots followed. Mood swings. Telling my boss what I really thought of him. Getting fired. And after all that, the cycle was canceled; I wasn't producing enough eggs.

The specialist said he didn't think in vitro fertilization would work for me after all—but I didn't believe him, couldn't believe him. I cried and cried.

Unfortunately, we hadn't spent quite all of our money. I found the biggest, the best, the most expensive doctor in all of L.A., who promptly shunted me over to his wife, a beginner with the bedside manner of a lizard. They claimed they could "fix" me. Jay administered more needles and love. We played more guitar songs to the infant spirit and felt so sad for the little baby lost out there in the dark. Another canceled cycle.

We tried one more time. Who needed to live in a house in Los Angeles? We could do without. Halfway through the cycle of shots I got a call from the nurse. She said to come in for an ultrasound. This bolstered my hopes. It meant they thought something good was going on.

So I jetted down there and was ushered into a dark little room lit only by the eerie green from the screen of the ultrasound machine. I dropped my drawers, wrapped myself in a sheet, and read *Better Homes & Gardens*. It was full of articles about how to fix up the home we could no longer afford. I was so excited. The wife of the bigwig came in (I hadn't seen the bigwig himself since my first multi-hundred-dollar consult). "Well," she said, slapping me on the knee, "the test was a washout. You're not going to have a baby unless you want to sign up for our egg donor program. Do you want to sign up for our egg donor program?"

Something deep inside of me, beyond the pain and close to the memory of our last bank statement, uttered a shaky "No." She left me alone in the dark room as I tried not to cry but to get my clothes on so I could get to my car where I could cry in peace and go home.

But no. "Mrs. Dougherty, you have to pay your bill before you leave." They sensed I wouldn't be back. After paying them thousands, my bill was now a few hundred. It was only eight in the morning. I had no checks on me. I was trying so hard not to cry. The bookkeeper was thoughtfully situated in full view of the crowded waiting room. She all but blockaded the exit until I found a check shriveled at the bottom of my purse for an account with a zero balance. I wrote it out anyway.

As I drove home I knew that my experience with hi-tech fertility treatments was over. I was relieved. Devastated, but relieved. A door had closed. We wouldn't have children. I was glad we didn't have any more money to spend. We'd go to Europe, we'd sleep late, we'd get a puppy. Just as soon as we finished paying that hospital bill. I was now thirty-nine. And no baby.

During my five-year addiction to the miracles of fertility science, not one of the medical whiz kids I consulted said anything about adoption. No one did except my mother. I should have been paying *her* thousands of dollars, her and my long-time gynecologist, Dr. Newman, who gave me a good talking to. "Open your heart to the possibility of adoption," Dr. Newman said. "Talk it over with Jay." Again I told him to bug off. The kind of baby I wanted didn't just come along every day. But I did

talk it over with Jay, and he was receptive.

The next day I was at my desk, looking out my office window at a lady pigeon that lived on the ledge. She was rustling around like she couldn't get comfortable, and then I saw the two baby birds under her, poking their beaks out. The mama stuck her beak in their feathers, fluffing them up, and dropped a bit of food into their tiny mouths. She looked so happy. At that moment, I knew we would adopt a child.

When the phone rang, it was Dr. Newman. "Are you sitting down?" he asked. He told me he had a young woman in his office, five months pregnant, blonde hair, blue eyes, looked like me. Were we interested? The world stood still. My search was reduced to a pinpoint of certainty. I knew at last where our baby was, and I said, "Yes."

Without looking, without trying, we were in the adoption loop. From this moment on, a layer of spirituality entered our lives. As our baby got closer to us, Jay and I got closer to each other. Not wanting to get my hopes up too high, I bought only one pair of baby socks.

But the money. What about the money? I sat on our bed, flipping through my address book, praying for an angel. And there, on the last page, was the name of an older gentleman we hadn't seen in a while. I got up my nerve and called him. We had lunch. It was hard to tell him how much I had always wanted a baby and how low our cash reserves were. Two little girls sat at the next table with their mother. I looked at them, then asked. He said, "I'll do it." With a smile.

When Bettina first appeared at our door, we looked at each other and took a step back; she could have been my niece. There were magic moments of coincidence. Every step fell into place, when things could so easily have fallen off track.

Why did Bettina pick us over the seven other couples suggested by her lawyer? When we wrote her we included things that friends had suggested we leave out. "Don't tell her Jay's in a rock 'n' roll band. Don't tell her you work with gangs." But I put those things in the letter, and Bettina said it was those very things that made her want to meet us.

Adoption is a human route to finding your baby. It therefore requires humanity. It is not always, perhaps, fair. The birth mother comes to the table with a baby and leaves with nothing. The adoptive parents come to the table and leave with a baby. But no one likes to feel empty. One of the reasons Bettina gave up her baby was that she wanted a career. We found out what her dreams were, and then we pulled in a favor from an old boss and got her a dream job. She had that to look forward to. Granted, a job is not quite the same as a baby. But we were the ones dreaming about a baby; she was the one dreaming about a career.

We don't have a huge house. We don't have tons of money. It felt like Bettina picked us because she knew and we knew that the baby she was carrying belonged in our home, with us. As we came to believe that babies choose their parents, we began to feel with all our hearts that Bettina was a hero. Our baby needed a ride. Bettina was willing to drop her off for the rest of her life with us.

We watched the birth and took our baby home when she was ten hours old. I asked our birth coach if there was anyone else in L.A. as happy as we were. She said yes—other adoptive parents.

All the hand-wringing that goes on over having to have your baby biologically ends up meaning zero once you become involved in the adoption process. Everyone in the adoption loop was kind. My doctor performed divine matchmaking. Then he stayed on board the whole way, making sure Bettina was feeling okay and I wasn't interfering too much. Our adoption lawyer had an adopted son, so she cut right to the chase. Our therapist juggled all of our fears and hopes and gave us courage. She served as the birth coach and stayed up all night with Bettina at the hospital while her dog slept in her cold car. Three months later, she sent us a bill for seventy-five dollars. Our social worker was efficient and friendly. And best of all, there were no stirrups. No bright lights. No painful invasions.

I was three weeks away from my fortieth birthday, and we had our baby.

It Took Three to Make a Family

CHERYL AND STEVE CLIFFORD
NORTH CANTON, OHIO

WHEN STEVE AND I GOT MARRIED, I was already forty and felt that my child-bearing years were behind me. Steve was only thirty-five and wanted a family, but ultimately he felt that being with me was more important than having children. After two incredibly happy years with Steve, I began to think I had been too hasty in my decision not to have children. As an associate pastor at my church, I had spent a lot of time with young kids and really enjoyed being with them. I broached the subject with Steve, telling him that I really did want to be a mother. He was ecstatic, and we started trying to get pregnant that very night.

When prospective parents put off trying to conceive until their forties, the possibility of getting pregnant in due time decreases dramatically. When Cheryl Clifford got married at age forty she was absolutely certain that she didn't want to have children. But things change. Four years later she and her husband, Steve, were fighting the infertility battle. When several cycles of fertility drugs failed to result in a pregnancy, the Cliffords turned to Cheryl's much younger sister for help.

Two long and very frustrating years later we still had not been able to conceive. By the time we consulted a fertility doctor, I was forty-five and Steve was forty. Months of treatments failed. When we turned to in vitro fertilization, I was forty-eight. Although our doctor felt I was healthy enough to carry a baby to term

24

if I became pregnant, he was very concerned about the viability of my eggs. He told us that the success rate for in vitro fertilization using eggs from a woman my age was only 3 percent. Steve and I didn't like those odds, so we decided to use the eggs of a woman under thirty, which would increase our chance of success by a factor of ten. Our doctor offered to locate a donor for us, but we really wanted the donor's genes to be similar to our own. He suggested that we consider a relative, adding that our chances of success would then be even better. Steve and I looked at each other and said in unison, "Heidi!"

Heidi is my sister, who was then twenty-eight years old. Heidi and I were always very close, even though I was in college when she was born. I would even sometimes pretend that she was my baby. Because she suffers from endometriosis, she may never be able to carry a child of her own. We didn't want her to help us if it would be too emotionally or physically trying for her, but decided to call her at home in Connecticut to explore the possibility. After consulting with her doctor about possible side effects of taking fertility drugs, she said that she absolutely wanted to do this for us. She told me, "In a strange sort of way, this somehow seems like my opportunity to conceive."

Heidi immediately started taking fertility drugs, and I began taking hormones to coordinate my cycle with hers. I wanted to be physically ready when Heidi's eggs were at their most fertile. Three weeks later, after her eggs had developed, Heidi flew to Ohio to have them retrieved by our doctor. Eight eggs were harvested, of which four were implanted inside me.

Two weeks later our doctor called us with the wonderful news that we were pregnant. We immediately called Heidi; I think we were all crying on the telephone. Still cautious, we went in for a follow-up visit two weeks after that, and an ultrasound revealed four living embryos. We were absolutely shocked and had read enough to know that all four babies might not make it. A high-risk-pregnancy specialist raised the possibility of aborting one or two of the embryos to help ensure the other's survival, but because of our religious beliefs that was not an option for us. We were told about the risks of multiple births for the babies (blindness, lung problems, even brain damage) and the mother (diabetes or high blood pressure), but there was never a doubt that we would take the risks.

At twenty weeks I was again put on bed rest, to prevent early labor. Three months later I had gained forty-six pounds and couldn't force down any more food, so the doctor decided to deliver the babies by cesarean section. On February 18, 1996, six weeks premature, Ruth, Paul, Robert, and namesake Heidi Lynn were born. As we only had a few hours notice before going to the hospital, Heidi couldn't attend the delivery, but we were on the phone with her as soon as I was physically able to talk.

Heidi is a very special part of the children's lives. We have kept a scrapbook of all the articles written about our family and share it regularly with her. She visits us as often as possible and has her own photo album of them growing up.

Parenting four babies is something like a huge strategic planning jigsaw—hopefully a facsimile of a family comes together at the end of the day. My mom now lives with us, and over sixty volunteers have come through our house. We are truly sharing our children with dozens of different people. Indeed, part of the joy we get from our children is seeing the joy they bring to others. After all, it took three—two parents who love them dearly and an exceptional aunt—to make their journey into this world possible.

Gifts

FRANCIS THADDEUS SEFCHIK, COLONEL USAF, RET.

PASSAIC, NEW JERSEY

RETIREMENT. What a strange word for a time so rich with new opportunity! With my air force career behind me, I was eager to move on to new ventures. One path led me to volunteer at a group home for troubled adolescents in the large urban area that was my home. My just being present and showing a sincere interest was, for some of these boys, a novel experience. The experience was an eye-opener for me, too.

I love to write. I had just completed a short story about a boy who was mistreated while in foster care and, in despair, ran away. A man who found and helped him cared for him and ultimately adopted him. It was a story about two people who became a happy, productive family—sort of a Horatio Alger story with an adoption twist. When I finished editing my manuscript, it was clear to me that it could be *my* story, that

By most standards Frank Sefchik, at sixty-eight, has led a full and rich life. His distinguished military career spanned thirty years and took him to every continent on earth. His awards, medals, and decorations for service could fill a wall. However, in retirement he longed to pursue the things that as a younger man he had sacrificed to the service of his country: he longed to have a family of his own. Was he "too old"? As the idea grew, so did his hopes. The length to which a man will go to become a father is the stuff of stories. Here is Frank's.

I could do at least as well as the father I had created in my story. Pondering this revelation, I decided that I could adopt, I should adopt, I would adopt. Thus began my journey and a new chapter in my life. I contacted close to one hundred agencies and found some who were willing to consider my case, despite my age, on the strength of homestudy evaluations. And I shared my hopes and dreams with my niece and her family, who embraced my decision enthusiastically and agreed to be my son's legal guardians should the need ever arise.

Almost one year later I received a fax that spelled out the good news: I was going to be allowed to adopt as my son seven-year-old Dima, removed from his parents when he was two and raised in a Siberian orphanage. The date for the adoption was set. The message also included an unusual request: would I please appear in uniform before the judge of the adoption court? Apparently, I had been represented as a compassionate colonel, and the officials in Siberia felt I was doing this child a favor by adopting him. Imagine! The fax ended with the observation, "Can you believe this, after all the years of the Cold War?" For me, this only proved what I have always said. People everywhere are basically the same. My years of service had earned me respect and a feeling of accomplishment. Now that same service was helping me to achieve my heart's

desire. No medal or commendation could ever equal this greatest reward, the gift of a son.

Adoption consists of many gifts freely given. For me, the first gift was the search that led me to my son—a journey born of deep, delayed longing that could no longer be set aside. The second gift was the act of adoption, which for Dima yielded a loving and caring father and for me the realization of a dream—a child to love and raise. The third gift was a name offered, combining both our names: Francis Thaddeus Dimitri Sefchik. Another gift was the unqualified support of an extended family of aunts, uncles, and cousins. And finally, there was the gift of U.S. citizenship, which will allow him every chance to become all that he can be and to accomplish all the good that he can do.

Adoption is a profound experience. As we waited in the courthouse in Russia, the adoption papers were typed, signed, and sealed in less than forty-five minutes, and Francis Thaddeus Dimitri Sefchik became my son. One week later, he set foot for the first time on American soil. And in no time at all we arrived at home, *our* home. It was exactly one year to the day since I had first dared to believe that adoption was possible. Now, on this day, Dima had a father, I had a son, and we were a family. For me, all else in my life has paled into insignificance.

Jacob Shares

ROB AND LAURA MAINS

DOVER, NEW JERSEY

"I DON'T WANT TO SHARE." This is one of two-and-a-half-year-old Jacob's favorite pronouncements. Yet he shares all the time, and it is because of sharing that we are a family. Each day, he shares a smile or a silly face. He looks at us with his bright blue eyes as he dances around the house, pretending to swim in an ocean, fly in the sky, or chug down a train track. He shares his rich imagination and his contagious laughter. He shares the joy he sees every day, without knowing how much all of his sharing means to those around him.

How many adults does it take to make a new family? For Rob and Laura Mains, the answer was four: two to conceive and carry the baby, two to raise the baby in strength and love, and all four to contribute to the child's sense of self. Rob and Laura's story proves once again that the path to parenthood is never clear-cut; though they set out in search of a traditional closed adoption with no threat of "interference" from the birth parents, it was Chris and Michelle who responded to the down-to-earth "Dear Birth Mother" letter they had written and who brought them Jacob.

When we were in the hospital meeting his birth mother, Michelle, for the first time as she prepared for Jacob's birth, we all had time to talk and learn about the reverence for life we all shared. Labor is a challenge, and we went through it together. It seems that allowing others to become part of his life from the very

start runs in Jacob's genes. It is not all that often that a hopeful adoptive mother gets the chance to cut the umbilical cord of her son-to-be; Michelle offered that to us. The generous heart and kind words of Chris, the birth father, are evident in the pages of Jacob's baby book and are made more real by the pictures he has shared of himself as a baby and a boy growing up.

It is ironic that Chris and Michelle, who in their wisdom and assessment of their own needs have given us life's ultimate gift, thanked *us* for accepting that gift. We continue to include Jacob's birth parents in his life, while remaining sensitive to the changes that invariably occur as people grow and their lives take new directions. There is an unwritten honor code that says if any one of us becomes uncomfortable with this arrangement, we will tell the others. In this way, Jacob will always have a large, extended family—a history with no secrecy or lies.

Anyone looking through our old family albums can see that Jacob strongly resembles how we looked as children and could pass as our biological child. This being the case, does anyone even need to know that he is adopted? When a passerby, drawn to Jacob's bubbly antics or wise observations, approaches us and mentions how much our son looks like us, we can agree that he does look like his parents, and wink knowingly at each other. The fact of Jacob's adoption clearly has no place in such casual encounters. But as teachers, openly sharing Jacob's story with the children in our middle school can be a powerful tool for their own understanding of a complex issue. Of course, the fact that Jacob is our real live son, not some textbook example, makes his story even more interesting. Most of the kids have a hard time imagining how they would feel if faced with the decision made by Chris and Michelle. However, seeing the circle of joy that radiates around Jacob as he strolls the halls definitely seems to influence their thinking in a positive way. For those students who also joined their families through adoption, there is a sense of pride and excitement in knowing that there are teachers at their school who really understand how some things can be both the same, yet different, when you are adopted. Once again, Jacob is sharing without even knowing it!

It took many years and many prayers for Jacob to find his way to our house. Complex as it may sound to others, his family is a simple fact to grasp: our son has four parents who love him. Two are with him physically, and all four are with him spiritually. Is it possible to have too much love? We do not think so. Our contact with Chris and Michelle will enhance our son's life.

"Resolving" Infertility

LISA AND GREG OSTRAVICH

HIGHLANDS RANCH, COLORADO

Infertility is often seen as a women's issue. In seeking solutions for their infertility, the Ostravichs confronted the reality that both women and men are vulnerable to the problem. With the help of an infertility support group where they could voice their fears and frustrations, they found a solution that worked for them.

GREG: Like many healthy men in their early thirties, I found it difficult to admit that I had a flaw. We had to go through in vitro fertilization to create Zachary, as my sperm count was so low. People usually think it is the woman who is infertile, but in reality almost 40 percent of all men have infertility problems as well. When Lisa finally got pregnant, one of my male coworkers asked me jokingly if the pregnancy was an accident. Nothing could have been further from the truth. Almost none of my male friends had any idea of the two long and frustrating years we went through to finally conceive our son.

LISA: We needed to know that we were not alone in our infertility heartbreak, so we went to an infertility group called Resolve for education and support. There we met other couples who were going through the same frustrations, and several lucky soon-to-be parents. I can't overemphasize the value of going to a support group during such a difficult time. Conception is supposed to be so easy and nat-

his staff determine that in vitro fertilization was what (hopefully) would work for us. Once we decided on in vitro fertilization we were both excited and scared. We met another couple at a Resolve meeting who had just gone through the process. They were not pregnant yet, and they told us about the drugs and shots and how uncomfortable and painful it sometimes was. But I didn't care.

GREG: When the medical staff did a complete physical and workup on me, they found out that my sperm count was really low; that was probably why Lisa couldn't get pregnant. This is something that most men don't want to talk about, as they feel that infertility is a direct hit on their virility, but male infertility can be overcome with the high technology available today. We tried the drug Clomid, and when my count increased a little the doctor recommended we try EXEY, an egg retrieval technique. I feel uncomfortable talking about it even now, but it is a process that men need to know about. I had to face the reality that I was probably shooting blanks. Sperm was injected into the petri dish in the laboratory, and we hoped that the eggs would be fertilized. Lisa was then injected with five fertilized eggs, and we started to play the waiting game.

ural, but when you're faced with infertility, every newborn baby you see is like a knife in your heart. Growing up I just assumed that I would get married and start a family in my early thirties, and when that didn't happen I began to wonder what was wrong with me. It took me a long time to realize infertility is not a defect but a medical problem that can sometimes be overcome.

I am a very impatient person, and after trying naturally to get pregnant for a year, I decided to go to a fertility specialist. Tests helped the doctor and

LISA: Even though I was injected with so many eggs, there was only a 2 percent chance of a single pregnancy, but at that point we didn't care. We were very excited about the possibility of finally being pregnant and never even seriously considered the possibility of multiple births, even though four women in our Resolve group were then pregnant with triplets. I just wanted a baby and didn't care if we had one or two children. We never thought about the possibility of more than two. After two weeks we went back for a pregnancy test. Our elation was dampened by the nurse, who prepared us for the worst. I was pregnant, but I had such a low HCG count that she thought I probably wouldn't be able to carry the baby to term. I had to go back to the hospital every two days for a week to see if my HCG count would double. It did.

GREG: Lisa went into premature back labor at twenty-two weeks and was put on bed rest for four days, but she was able to carry Zachary to term. We had a scare, however, when we learned that his feet were tucked inside and he had to go on a fetal monitor just to make sure he was still moving. An ultrasound revealed that everything was just fine. Lisa and I now feel so lucky; we have several relatives who tried unsuccessfully to get pregnant at the same time we did. Most people are not aware of how common infertility is. When we tell people

about conceiving Zachary through in vitro fertilization, everyone assumes that it was Lisa who had the difficulty conceiving, when in fact the problem was with me. Zachary is such an amazing baby. We had to go through two such difficult years to bring him into this world. He was truly created by tremendous love and perseverance.

LISA: One of the most wonderful things about my pregnancy was that my sister got pregnant several weeks after I did. It happened so easily for her, but I had been trying for so long that we had quite a celebration. We live very near each other. Since I opted to be a stay-at-home mom, I take care of both boys. It's just like having twins, without having to have given birth to them both.

Infertility will always be an issue in our lives and a problem we will have to deal with. We plan on having another baby and will have to conceive by in vitro fertilization again. But Resolve will help us get through it. It has always been important for me to do something meaningful in my life, and what could be more important than working with an organization that gives encouragement, support, and valuable information to so many people who so deeply want to be parents?

A Family of Four

TOM AND YOLANDE GASBECK
SIMI VALLEY, CALIFORNIA

Infertility often leads to confusion and indecision. Adoption or medical intervention? Which to pursue? Tom and Yolande Gasbeck chose both, first adopting a daughter from China and then welcoming a son born to them through high-tech means. The journey for each child was arduous and emotional, but the outcome was well worth it.

YOLANDE: I vividly remember the day we decided to adopt a child from China. Tom and I were invited to a Christmas party hosted by a woman who owned an international adoption agency. There were families with children from all over the world—China, India, Russia, Vietnam, and Latin America. It was the Chinese baby girls that caught my eye and heart. Being Chinese myself, it was amazing to see so many children who looked like me. I felt an immediate identification and kinship with them. Seven months later we were in China, bringing home four-month-old Katie.

TOM: Children have always been important to us, and we spent two very tough years trying to conceive. After a year of trying to conceive naturally, Yolande started on the fertility drug Clomid, got pregnant, and miscarried three months later. Our lives became an emotional roller coaster ride that revolved around determining when Yolande was fertile, going to the doctor to get inseminated, and then waiting to find out if she was pregnant. Our fertility specialist then tested me and found out that my sperm count was so low I was essentially infertile. When Yolande miscarried, I began to think that perhaps God had another plan for us. Our choices were to try in vitro fertilization or to seriously start exploring adoption options. China made the most sense for us. My wife and in-laws were born in Hong Kong, and I was excited to begin exploring their cultural and historical roots.

YOLANDE: There was never any doubt in our minds that if we were going to adopt internationally, we would go to China. Besides my obvious ties to the country, we wouldn't fear having our child reclaimed once we had her. After going through a miscarriage, we couldn't bear the thought of possibly losing another baby. We had heard such wonderful things about the Chinese program and about how healthy most of the babies are. Being in China was a bittersweet experience for me. Luckily, my parents had been able to leave the country to give our family a better chance at life. But when I saw how it is there, standing right where it all started and seeing so many people living in shacks, I realized that Katie could have been me thirty years ago. It really hit me how different China is from the United States. If we hadn't adopted our daughter, I might never have fully understood my own good fortune, and she might never have had a chance for a better life.

TOM: We knew that we would be able to give Katie a good education, superior health care, and lots of love and attention. It was so sad to know that thousands of newborn baby girls die each year in China. When the three of us returned to California—on the Fourth of July weekend—and started to settle in, we realized how lucky we are to live in this country. After we got home Yolande and I suffered from jet lag and had problems sleeping for several nights. But Katie, bless her, slept through the night from day one. She was and is such a great little girl.

YOLANDE: Eighteen months after returning from China, we decided to try to get pregnant again. This time it was a much more relaxed and enjoyable experience. I took a new kind of fertility drug and was inseminated with donor sperm, but the pressure was not so intense. If I couldn't conceive, it wouldn't break my heart the way it had two years earlier, when I was inseminated six times and didn't get pregnant. I was only twenty-nine and Tom was thirty-four when we adopted Katie, and we realized that we had many years ahead of us. Besides, we already had a beautiful child.

Who could have guessed that I would become pregnant! Throughout this difficult pregnancy, I thought a lot about what Katie's birth mother must have been thinking when she was pregnant. How did she feel about giving her up, and why did she do it? At seven months I was put on strict bed rest and was constantly torn between Katie's needing me and having to be in bed to keep from losing Tommy. It was a very hard and emotional time for me, as I couldn't even pick my daughter up when she cried.

TOM: It was a very difficult time for all three of us. I tried to help Yolande as much as I could, and our neighbors were terrific, helping with meals and even cleaning our house. Yolande was taken off bed rest at thirty-six weeks and went into a very difficult labor several days later. But little Tommy was born a perfect baby. Being an infertile male, I really feel lucky to have a healthy and beautiful boy and girl. They give me a sense of unity, responsibility, and accomplishment.

YOLANDE: Anyone who goes through infertility lives day by day. When I was living through it I thought we would never have a family. My children are a true blessing, a joy as well as a sacrifice. I think I am a much better mother than I would have been without the experiences we've had. What I wanted most in life was two children, and now we have them. Although Tom and I took alternative paths to get our children—adoption and assisted conception—they both led to the same wonderful outcome.

It Took a Village

FRED GOHL AND TRACI SHAHAN-GOHL

HIGHLANDS RANCH, COLORADO

TRACI: Our journey began when I was a naive twenty-year-old college student. During a routine gynecological appointment I was told that I would probably be unable to bear children because I had been born with an abnormally shaped uterus. I did not grow up desiring marriage or children, so I took the news calmly. In fact, in a way I was relieved, as it meant I would not have to explain my lifestyle as a choice; rather, my childless state resulted from an unlucky shuffle of the DNA deck. That mind-set persisted until my dear friend Steve died. After having devoted most of his adult life to the demanding profession of medicine, Steve left this planet far too early. I was consoled by his having left a namesake, or as I like to think, a "soulsake," in the form of his nine-year-old son. The strong realization that I would not do the same hit with a fierce impact.

It's been said that it takes a village to raise a child. In the case of Traci and Fred, it took the help of a modern "village" to conceive their twin girls and bring them into the world through surrogacy. Hannah and Taylor, who were born in April 1997, came into being with the help, love, and support of Fred and Traci's embryologist, their physician, their pastor, and Sara, the babies' surrogate. Fred, who is a dentist and Traci, who is working on her doctorate in nursing, are now actively involved in the community that gave them crucial support.

FRED: Unlike Traci, I had always dreamed of having a family. I love children and believed that there was no more wonderful way to experience life completely than by raising a child. Because of my love for Traci, I always believed that she would have a change of heart and want a family, too. I had no idea how hard our struggle would be.

TRACI: When I lost a pregnancy after a four-year period of difficult conceptions, miscarriages, surgeries, and fertility medications, I vowed it would be my last. As Fred and I sat, brokenhearted and broken in spirit, my physician told me that even with the latest treatments and surgeries, I would probably never carry a pregnancy to term. This prognosis, from the man who had always encouraged us, rocked me to the core.

FRED: In the preceding year, Sara, who would become our surrogate, had begun writing to Traci, offering to "baby-sit for nine months." We had met Sara through mutual friends and continued to see her at gatherings, but we did not know her well.

At first the possible ramifications of traditional surrogacy, in which the carrier's egg is fertilized by the father's sperm, frightened us. But as we learned about in vitro fertilization surrogacy, in which the biological parents' egg and sperm are combined and the surrogate carries the child, we became more comfortable.

TRACI: Right after my last loss, Sara and her husband showed up at our house to drop off gifts and a book about adoption. When I realized that all Sara had wanted all along was for us to have children—by whatever means we felt comfortable with—I burst into tears, told the adoption agency to put our file on hold, and called Dr. Worley the next day to begin synchronizing my cycle with Sara's. The process of coordinating two women's cycles is intricate, uncomfortable, and time-consuming. It can also be very intimate. We knew when each other's periods would start, what injections each was taking, and how we were coping emotionally. Unlike those rare cases in which a child is conceived using a "turkey baster," in vitro fertilization surrogacy requires incredibly detailed medical protocols and mental toughness. It also requires large sums of money.

FRED: After seeing Traci go through so much, and when I thought I might lose her after a hemorrhage following surgery, I did not want her to endure more. But she and Sara had become very close and were there for each other during the uncomfortable procedures.

TRACI: After an initial scare of a miscarriage, Sara became ill with morning sickness that lasted all day and all night. There were times when she could not get out of bed, and in fact she was once hospitalized. I was powerless to ease her constant suffering and felt guilty watching her go through this for us. But she never complained. Several times each month we all met for obstetrician appointments and watched our twins via ultrasound. Invariably these appointments ended with hugs and tears of relief as we saw our girls moving and growing. Because I was working more than full-time on my doctorate in nursing we could not see each other as often as we wanted, so we talked on the phone and wrote long, powerful letters to each other.

The two girls were born amid chaos, during the worst snowstorm of the season. Sara made it to the hospital just before Hannah's umbilical cord prolapsed, compromising her oxygen supply. After an emergency C-section, our girls were born dusky blue but alive. Taylor improved, but Hannah got progressively worse. Because of pressure imbalances in her blood vessels, her delicate lungs started to hemorrhage, and her heart began to pump ineffectively. Time seemed to stop. Although she was sedated, we would touch her and whisper in her ear that we would never leave her and that she had to be strong. And although she lay eerily still, Hannah responded by wrapping her tiny hand around my index finger. After several days we finally started to see improvement.

We will never be able to repay our debt to Sara, but I am trying to give back through my work in the field of infertility. During this final year of my doctoral studies I am working with the practice where we received our fertility care, Conceptions Women's Health and Fertility Specialists. It is intensely gratifying to help others who are struggling with the same issues we did. Infertility is not only about the lack of a child, it's about the pain of giving up your life bit by bit—financially, emotionally, socially, professionally—for a chance to try for what comes easily to most others: creating a family.

FRED: Sara's courageous gift made us realize how critical it is for us to emphasize to our girls the importance of service to others and reverence for people in difficult circumstances—the importance of having compassion. I now have a reason to live that goes beyond my own aspirations and myself. Today, my most important job is to guard, honor, and nurture these precious lives.

TRACI: Our journey has truly been about the power of encountering and overcoming enormous challenges, not just through sheer individual determination but with the help of special people. It is a testament to the reality that human kindness and benevolence still exist in a society often characterized as apathetic and unkind. By all odds, our girls should not be here. Hannah Lee and Taylor Morgan are beautiful, gentle spirits, messengers of the truth that, in the final analysis, life is good.

Mimi and Grandpa

ROBERT AND EVELYNE McNAMARA

SAN JOSE, CALIFORNIA

The loss of a much-loved child is a devastating experience for a family. Bob and Evelyne McNamara decided to add to their family through adoption—not to replace the child they lost to cancer but in recognition of the joy that a child brings to a family. But what happens when not every member of the family is enthusiastically supportive?

MY HUSBAND AND I HAVE had four biological children. Our youngest daughter died of a brain tumor when she was four years old; our other three children are now nineteen, seventeen, and fourteen. My children adored their late sister, as did the rest of my extended family. My father, who was one of our daughter's primary caregivers, took her loss particularly badly. When we first began to consider adoption we spoke to our children about it, and their response was overwhelmingly positive. Enough time had passed for all of us to be clear that this new child would not be a replacement but, rather, a joyful late addition.

Three years later, we traveled to China to adopt our beautiful daughter Mimi, now two. My mother was diagnosed with breast cancer the same week that we began telling our family we were starting the adoption process. The anticipation of gaining a new grandchild—who was to be her namesake—helped give her focus during the anxious months in which she had a double mastectomy and

about "yellow peril." Now he was supposed to accept one as his grandchild?

Nothing we said as the months passed had any effect on his hard stance. Two weeks before leaving for China we called a family meeting, and tears in my eyes, I begged him to try not to reject the coming baby. I reminded him that I, her mother, had greatly loved and mourned his late granddaughter but that I was ready to love again and that this child, from my body or not, was coming. Would he try to accept her? Shamed at last, he told me to just let him have some time. He wasn't a monster, for heaven's sake. He wasn't going to hurt the baby. It was just that expecting him to be her grandfather was going too far.

We adopted Mimi on June 10, 1996, in Changsha, Hunan Province. Exquisite and affectionate, she so far exceeded our expectations that we were overwhelmed. We were reborn ourselves as parents and couldn't wait to share her with the whole family. Our children listened to every detail when we called to tell them about their new sister. My father refused to pick up the phone. My mother simply repeated my conversations with her, and grudgingly he began to be intrigued by this paragon we described.

After a grueling trip home we landed in California. My husband and I were drippy, sweaty messes. Mimi, however, with only five hours of sleep in twenty-nine hours of travel, was dressed in her

began her recovery. My father, in contrast, was unbendingly negative. His unspoken thoughts were plain. We were betraying his beloved granddaughter's memory by bringing in an interloper, and he refused to have anything to do with her. She would not be *his* grandchild, he baldly stated, not this Chinese stranger. And why Chinese, for heaven's sake! Couldn't we get some blond Irish kid if we had to do this stupid thing? In his day, people looked suspiciously at Asian faces and whispered

finest, happy as a clam, and ready to wow the waiting crowd. We stumbled off the plane and into the jetway. At the other end, having sneaked past the waiting crowd and the airline security cordon, was my father. My husband passed him with a "Hi," and my father barely acknowledged him. He stared at the baby as I approached. "Here she is," I said. Mimi studied him for a second, flashed a twenty-thousand-watt smile, then reached out and squeezed his nose. She's been leading him by it ever since.

It helps a lot that Mimi is unrelenting in her desire to conquer people who don't want to be charmed. In restaurants she looks around, selects a target, focuses her considerable attention on it, and then zaps the lucky individual with charm until he or she succumbs. My father didn't have a chance. Within weeks she was throwing herself into his arms whenever he was near. He began to take her outside to show her his koi pond and cockatiel. A born courtier, she thrills at the sight each time as if it were the first. Grandpa (oh yes, he most definitely answers to the title, especially since at ten months *Ampa* was her fourth word!) now takes her for walks around the neighborhood and introduces her proudly as his granddaughter. Her being Chinese is no longer a stigma in his eyes. Now it is just another feature that marks her as unique, for *his* grandchildren are never ordinary.

The other children's reactions have continued to be very positive. In fact, our fifteen-year-old daughter, who suffers from severe attention deficit–hyperactivity disorder and has had problems managing her anger and behavior, has been able to make significant positive changes since the baby came home because she wanted Mimi to have a home free from stress. None of us realized how much we missed the presence of a small child in our home. Together we shared a great loss, and together we celebrate this great joy—as a family.

POSTSCRIPT: In March 1998, another little girl from China joined the McNamara family. Named Cai, she was in the same foster home as Mimi, where they were raised together as "crib sisters."

Pass the Word

TOM AND BETSY CUNNEFF
MARINA DEL REY, CALIFORNIA

Whereas many adoption stories illustrate the experience of "hurry up and wait," Tom and Betsy Cunneff's took an atypical "wait and hurry up" twist when they began to investigate the possibility of adopting. Now the thrilled adoptive parents of three-year-old Katie, the Cunneffs are vivid proof of the good that can result from lifting the veil of secrecy from adoption.

TOM: Someone once told me that there are two types of people in this world: those with children and those without. Betsy and I always knew that we wanted children, but we never felt in any particular hurry, because we knew how drastically children would change our lifestyle. We had a great life together, traveling extensively using Betsy's benefits as a flight attendant. Perhaps that's why we tried to get pregnant on our own for a good two years before we finally went to see a fertility specialist.

BETSY: I have always been an optimist, and I just knew during those two years that I would get pregnant soon. But one day I had lunch with a friend who also happened to be a fertility counselor. When I told her how long we had been trying, she just looked at me and said, "You're in denial, Betsy. You have an infertility problem, and you need some help." I realized she was right. I hadn't wanted to face the reality that I might not be able to carry a child. But I was in my late

problems that were easily correctable. After taking large doses of fertility drugs, I then began the first of nine artificial inseminations.

TOM: Each time I was sure *this* would be the one that would work, but our hopes were always dashed a couple of weeks later. The frustrating part was that they couldn't tell us what the problem was. Frequently, all the specialists in the world can't pinpoint what the reason is, so you're constantly left in limbo. For 10 percent of all infertile couples, their infertility is "unexplained." We, unfortunately, fell into that category. I just remember it was very important that I not take a Jacuzzi or wear tight underwear or pants during those years, because it might adversely affect my sperm count. But that was about all they could tell us.

thirties, and I knew I had to deal with the problem. I knew it was going to be a long, expensive, and physically and emotionally uncomfortable experience to enter the world of infertility treatments. My friend, who had just given birth to her daughter by in vitro fertilization, referred me to her doctor—one of the top specialists in Los Angeles, with a highly respected clinic in Santa Monica. We spent three long years trying to conceive. First came a myriad of tests on both of us to isolate what the difficulty might be. There were a couple of minor

BETSY: After the ninth failed insemination attempt and thousands of dollars down the drain, we turned to a process called "GIFT," by which the sperm and eggs are placed by the doctor into the fallopian tube. We never made it to the operating table, however. Despite having three injections a day for a week at a time, I wasn't able to generate the necessary amount of eggs for the procedure. My ovaries had had enough, and so had I. Our next alternative was to use donor eggs, but I didn't want to be poked with one more needle, use anymore drugs, or endure anymore letdowns. We were not going to have our own biological child, and this was hard for me to deal with. But were we going to remain childless and continue to live our lives as we always had? Or could I move past the loss and think about loving a child I did not give birth to? It took me a good year and a lot of thinking before we could make the next step: adopting. One book that really helped was *Adopting After Infertility* by Patricia Johnston. I was very moved by a line in the book that said, "God doesn't close any doors without opening a window." It made me realize that it was time to let go of the past and move forward to create our family.

TOM: Our first step was to attend a two-night adoption seminar to learn about both domestic and international adoption. I remember sitting in this big room with about fifty other couples and thinking, "Oh my God. All these people want a baby, too. They're competition." It was a bit discouraging. But the one vital piece of advice we took away from it was not to keep our adoption plans a secret. The speaker encouraged us to ask anyone and everyone if they knew of somebody struggling with an unwanted pregnancy.

BETSY: Two weeks later a couple of dear friends from back East, Kathy and Doug, were visiting with us. While Tom and Doug were playing golf one morning, Kathy and I had a long heart-to-heart over breakfast. I was excited to tell her about our decision to adopt. I told her about the seminar and that we were in the midst of looking for an adoption lawyer. I then turned to her and said, half-jokingly, "So, do you know anyone who's pregnant?" Her eyes got as big as saucers as she realized that, yes, she did actually know of a teenage girl in her neighborhood. The family already knew they wanted to put the child up for adoption but had not yet chosen the adoptive couple.

TOM: After several letters and phone conversations, we flew back east to meet the birth mother and her family. It couldn't have gone better. We all clicked, and everyone felt this was the right thing to do for all concerned. A month later we got a predawn call telling us she had gone into labor nine days early. We were on a plane within a few hours and found out en route that we had a daughter. We saw her for the first time that evening in the hospital nursery.

BETSY: The next day, just outside the hospital, the birth mother placed Katie in my arms for the first time. I still can't believe how quickly and easily she came into our lives. A lot of people would call us lucky. But this was the baby we were meant to have. As soon as we opened up our hearts to her and pursued her, she came to us. I guess some things are just meant to be.

From We to Three

ROBYN AND SCOTT CAWOOD
MOUNT ARLINGTON, NEW JERSEY

SCOTT AND I HAVE BEEN MARRIED eight years. We both enjoyed our early married life: we traveled, worked on projects around the house, went out to dinner or the movies, and enjoyed the freedom of being a young, child-free couple. Eventually, however, we began to talk about having a baby and agreed that we were both ready to start a family. We knew that this would not be easily accomplished, as I had a medical condition that made conception all but impossible without the help of medical technology.

We read everything we could find on adoption and in vitro fertilization to help us with our decision. Cost was an issue, since our health insurance did not cover in vitro fertilization. The procedure was costly, the success rate was not great—there were no guarantees. To add to all that, we were worried about the stress it would put on our marriage if it failed. Both of us agreed that adoption was our answer.

They just wanted to hear a child call them Mommy and Daddy. Was that so much to ask for? Wanting something so badly and finding every path blocked is both frustrating and painful. The drain on personal finances only adds to the problem. Adoption seemed to offer them their best chance. Then Robyn's new health plan suddenly offered a second option: coverage for hi-tech fertility treatments. Adoption? Pregnancy? Now they actually had a choice.

We felt so alone as we explored various adoption avenues, until friends of ours successfully adopted a baby. Suddenly we had the support of someone else who truly understood the emotional roller coaster we were riding. We talked to them about how we should go about getting started, and we began researching several adoption agencies until we found one that fit our needs. Filled with joy and hope, we felt sure that a baby would soon join our family. We shared our excitement with our families, who called us frequently, eager to hear about each new development. But there was nothing to report. Despite our best preparation and planning, our efforts were leading us nowhere. There were a few promising leads that almost led to a placement, but things never quite worked out. It was a very difficult time, both for us and for our families. What was wrong with us? Why couldn't we become parents? We finally hit rock bottom. Through our two years of waiting to adopt, Scott and I clung bravely to our faith that God would bring into our lives—eventually—the baby we were meant to have.

It seemed clear that we would have to make some changes, so we started to look into other adoption agencies. Then my school district renegotiated our contract and switched to a new health insurance plan that would cover a significant portion of the costs of infertility treatment. Suddenly, it seemed, we had choices. We decided to cover all

bases: we would continue in the waiting-to-adopt loop while also trying in vitro fertilization. It felt right to us, and eagerly but nervously we moved forward again, in anticipation of parenthood. How we longed to be called Mommy and Daddy!

The rest is history. Friends recommended a clinic that had had success with other women with my medical condition, and we made an appointment. I was put on medication and had to visit the doctor weekly. On some days the ride to the clinic seemed endless. Scott and I prayed that we were doing the right thing and that it would work. Again, we shared what we were doing with family and friends and asked for their prayers and support. I belong to our church choir, and they, too, prayed for us. Everyone's love, support, and prayers helped us through the process.

On July 5, 1996, three fertilized eggs were implanted in my womb, and I was sent home on twenty-four hours bed rest—to wait. The next two weeks seemed to last forever. When I finally went back to the clinic on July 17 for a pregnancy test, I could only pray. Later that day we received the incredible news: we had beaten the odds, and I was pregnant! Our long journey seemed to be coming to an end. Although we still had some fear that something might go wrong, we felt that God had blessed this pregnancy and the little baby that was growing inside me.

It was a relatively smooth pregnancy. Everyone

was excited for us because they knew how hard we had worked to get pregnant and how badly we wanted to be parents. On March 21, 1997, at 8:15 A.M., Caitlin Marie entered the world. She has brought so much joy into our lives that I cannot even put it into words. Scott and I are enjoying being parents and feel truly blessed. Adoption or "hi-tech" pregnancy? When your primary desire is to parent a child, to become a family in the fullest sense, is one option better than the other in the end? Looking back, we would not have changed anything; this is the path God chose for us. We believe in miracles, because we look at one every day: Caitlin Marie Cawood!

Part II

The Wonder Years

....

*A*S THE CHILDREN OF FAMILIES FORMED in nonconventional ways enter the toddler years, the challenge and focus of parenting begins to change dramatically. How do you begin to explain to your children how they came into your lives and why their family is, perhaps, different from the families of their friends? The newness of becoming parents, either again or for the first time, has started to wear off. Although still in the "wonder years," these families are now facing concerns that more traditional families generally do not have to deal with. Their children are now old enough to understand when a well-meaning but insensitive stranger asks at the supermarket, "Where did your child come from?" or "Where are his *real* parents?" The idealistic and unique path taken by these parents to bring children into their lives now leads those children on an unorthodox journey of their own.

The stories in this section tell the experiences of families created by domestic and international adoption, in vitro fertilization, and donor insemination. Family groupings are varied, and include traditional two-parent households as well as families headed by a single parent and others by same-sex couples. Single parenthood is a daunting responsibility, especially during the toddler years, when the need to work to support a child usually involves finding suitable day care. A single mother struggles to find a way to tell her six-year-old son, conceived through donor insemination, who and where his father is. A single father who has finally come to terms with his sexuality has just adopted a second child and is raising them both on his own. And when two single parents with children get married, creating a blended family presents its own set of unique challenges.

At this age, racism and prejudice have started to rear their ugly heads. Parents who adopt across racial lines may find their children targets of racial discrimination at school. Sexual orientation is no longer an issue in becoming parents, but same-sex couples are starting to realize that their children may experience discrimination at school because of their parents' lifestyle.

Yes, the excitement and wonder of being a new parent has begun to wear off, and the reality and concerns these nontraditional families face have set in. At times they are traveling a bumpy road filled with tough questions and difficult answers. But all these families are experiencing parenthood with joy, love, and hope.

Jordan's Story

SUZZANNE DOUGLAS AND ROY COBB

MAPLEWOOD, NEW JERSEY

For a public figure, the decision to adopt can result in an intrusive and sometimes hurtful barrage of questions. Suzzanne, a successful actress, was frequently hounded not only by the press but also by complete strangers about her inability to conceive. In seeking to adopt her daughter, Jordan, she perceived bias against adoption within the African-American community as well as a fear among men of dealing honestly with infertility.

A S AN AFRICAN-AMERICAN ACTRESS living in Los Angeles, years of infertility and the adoption process have presented a unique set of challenges for me. Roy and I were hounded by complete strangers and members of the press as well as by friends and relatives concerning when we were going to have children, first, and then why we couldn't have children. Later they wanted to know why we decided to adopt and who Jordan's "real" mother is. I made my answers simple. We adopted Jordan because we wanted a child. Her real parents are an actress and a doctor—me and Roy.

But my having a high-profile career made it hard at the beginning for the foster mother who kept Jordan while we were waiting for the adoption to become final. She told her family and friends that Jordan was being adopted by "that actress on *The Parenthood,*" and she told me she sat Jordan down in front of the television set as a newborn to watch my show. When we came to pick up

Jordan all I wanted was to take our baby home and start to bond with her. We took her away from everything. We took her to our home on Martha's Vineyard.

It is difficult to talk about the pain and heartbreak of infertility. Our doctor could not find a biological problem with either Roy or me; for some reason we just could not make a baby together. I was on an emotional roller coaster for five years and began wearing black all the time. When I started to take fertility drugs my weight skyrocketed and I experienced severe mood swings. I felt so overwhelmed by my own loss that I couldn't be happy for my friends when they told me they were pregnant, and I cried in desperation at baby showers. A relative gave me sexy lingerie and tried to tell me how to make love to my husband. Our doctor finally said that location could be the problem, as I was in Los Angeles working on my television series and Roy was practicing in New Jersey. In simple terms, we were never together.

Roy and I always wanted both a biological and an adopted child to complete our family, so we were in the domestic adoption process during this time. When the placement of a baby boy fell through when his birth mother changed her mind, I began to think that I was never going to be a mother. In the African-American community there is a real stigma about adopting baby boys due to the fear of gangs and police brutality, but baby girls are always at a pre-mium. We didn't care about the sex of our baby; we just wanted a child. There is also a lot of fear and mistrust in the African-American community regarding adoption in general. Many men believe that not being able to conceive a child is a direct hit on their manhood and refuse to deal with the problem or consider adoption. But by the same token, there is also strong concern over biracial adoptions and the fear that Caucasian parents won't be sensitive to an African-American child's culture and heritage. I strongly disagree with this attitude. Every child needs a warm and caring home, regardless of the color of his or her skin, and black history can be discovered at libraries, museums, and cultural events.

After the disappointment of losing that baby boy, I was ready to start in vitro fertilization. Then our agency called. They had a birth mother who thought we might be a good match. Roy and I had written biographies of ourselves and created a photo collage depicting our extended family, sports we played, and other activities we loved. When the birth mother chose us we cried and hugged each other. I looked a lot like her, and since she didn't watch television, she didn't know who I was, which was just great. She was a college-bound high school senior who grilled us about our home situation and our plans for the baby's education. This was a young girl who truly loved her soon-to-be-born child and knew she would be cared for, nurtured, and loved in our home.

Jordan was born and placed immediately in foster care. Seven weeks later she was in our arms for good. We became a family, and I saw life in its purest, most unadulterated form. This must be the way that God loves us: unconditionally. Our lifestyle hasn't changed; it has been enriched with Jordan's arrival. She is a welcome addition to our family and our circle of friends. She is in a loving environment and is learning about life, mistakes and all, in a protected world.

One of the most important lessons Jordan has to learn is about giving. I want her to be a giver and not a taker. It is also important for Jordan to know and understand about diversity, as she will be living and growing in many different worlds. I really think that the adoption world is starting to change, becoming much more open and liberal. Yet so many of these questions still hurt us deeply. There is frequently the assumption that African-American women who place their babies for adoption must be fifteen-year-old drug addicts. Both the press and questioning strangers want to assume that it is always an ugly situation, when nothing could be further from the truth. Jordan's birth parents loved her deeply, and because of this love, they gave us a jewel to raise and to guide.

The rest is Jordan's story, and when she is ready to tell it, she will.

My Two Children from China

Paul Montz

Phoenix, Arizona

Not until he found the courage to leave his marriage and confront his sexuality was Paul Montz finally able to realize his dream of having a family. Juggling single parenthood with two children under the age of four and a demanding career is exhausting, he says, but also exhilarating and fulfilling.

I LOOK BACK AT THE LAST FOUR YEARS of my life in absolute amazement. A single forty-year-old man, I am now the proud father of a son and daughter, something that in my early thirties I thought might never happen. It took me several years of soul-searching and therapy to realize that I didn't have to be married or straight to be a good father.

My initial desire to be a parent began when I was a young boy. I had one of those wonderful, almost idyllic childhoods. Growing up on a farm in Dover, Delaware, I always felt supported by my parents, who let me be my own person and gave me unconditional love. This is why I so strongly wanted to be a parent—to pass on to my own children the happiness and security I had been blessed with as a child.

Having remained single well into my thirties, and still not having come to grips with my sexual orientation, I began to fear that parenthood would not be possible. I made the decision to get married and found a like-minded partner.

Never deeply in love, we nevertheless shared a common goal—to give birth to a child. After two years of trying we were unable to conceive and underwent fertility treatments for the next year. All our conversations had to do with having a child, and eventually the stress, frustration, and devastation drove us apart. I wanted so deeply to be a father and was extremely caught up by the ideal of having a biological connection to my children. As for my wife, it was only our shared goal of conceiving a child that had brought us together, and I found I could not continue in a marriage that was falling apart.

After our divorce I fell into a deep depression as I confronted my horrible fear that fatherhood was not going to happen for me. After more than a year of therapy and grieving over the loss of the child I never had, I began to realize that there was another option—adoption. But having grown up in such a happy two-parent family, I was terrified of doing it alone.

At this point I began to realize that getting married again was not an option and that I had some serious choices to make. At first I thought only about domestic adoption, as I wanted a child who would look like my biological offspring. Perhaps deep down inside I didn't want people to know my child had been adopted. But I soon found out that trying to adopt domestically as a single man is almost impossible. I had a lot of doors slammed in

my face. So not only did I have to open myself up to the possibility of adoption, it now looked like my only choice was to go international. My child would not look like me; I had to ask myself if I could truly love it. Yes, I decided, I could!

I thought I would be a better parent to a girl, though I didn't really know why. I admired the beauty of Asian people, and China became an obvious choice, as almost all of the children available for adoption there are female. When I was eventually approved, I began to dream about my beautiful baby girl. Then came the midnight call that I will never forget. My Chinese facilitator asked me how I would feel about getting a boy. There is a law on the books in China, unknown to most people who want to adopt, that forbids single people under forty from adopting opposite-sex babies. I was flabbergasted; there had never been any doubt in my heart and mind that I was meant to be the father of a daughter. I had been thinking "girl" for eight months, and this revelation took some gear switching. But the bottom line was this: I wanted a child.

I was thirty-eight at the time my application was approved, so at first China turned me down. China does not give up its boys easily. Not only was I not going to get a daughter, there was a strong chance that I would not get a baby at all. This was a bleak time in my life. Thankfully, my facilitator found a baby boy who had been hidden in an orphanage and sent me his picture. It was love at first sight—I knew that this child was *my* son. Ten days later, on December 30, 1994, I was on a plane to China.

"Oh my God, he looks Chinese," was my enlightened response when this five-month-old baby boy was placed in my arms, and I started to cry. By the end of the first day he had a name, Chad, and he was all mine, my son. The practical, routine aspects of parenting—bathing a baby, changing diapers, bottle-feeding—were all unfamiliar to me, and it has been an incredible learning experience. Two weeks after returning home from China I dropped my son on his head. He was fine, but I wasn't for weeks. And as Chad gets older the challenges become more complex, especially because I am doing it alone. I now realize that all the wonderful things Mom and Dad did for me came at a price.

Last year, when Chad turned three, I began to feel that there was another child out there for me. In late October I went back to China and brought eight-month-old Carly home. During the adoption process my agency told me that as I already had a child from China, I had to be open to the possibility that my second child would have special needs. The child referred to me, I was informed, was deaf, but that didn't matter to me. Luckily it turned out that Carly had been mis-diagnosed and her hearing is just fine. However, two other families that were traveling with me to adopt second children got babies with correctable disabilities.

All my friends told me that a second child is more than twice the work, but I actually find that Chad and Carly play with each other and give me an occasional break. Sometimes I feel there is not enough of me to go around, but my own parents have been a great help to me during the busiest times, visiting often and giving my kids, their grandchildren, all the love and nurturing they gave me growing up. I am confident that I can give Chad and Carly the same kind of wonderful start in life that my parents gave me.

Everyone has his own process to go through before becoming a parent. For me it was changing my sights from becoming a biological parent to being an adoptive one. The adoption process was the pregnancy, and the labor was going to China. We all have a purpose in life, and I know that the purpose in my life is to be Chad's and Carly's daddy. I used to think that the ideal family was two children, a mother and father, and material things. Boy, have I changed in the last three years! Now a family means love, support, guidance, and learning. I take it in stride—parenting is my job and my calling. We need and love one another.

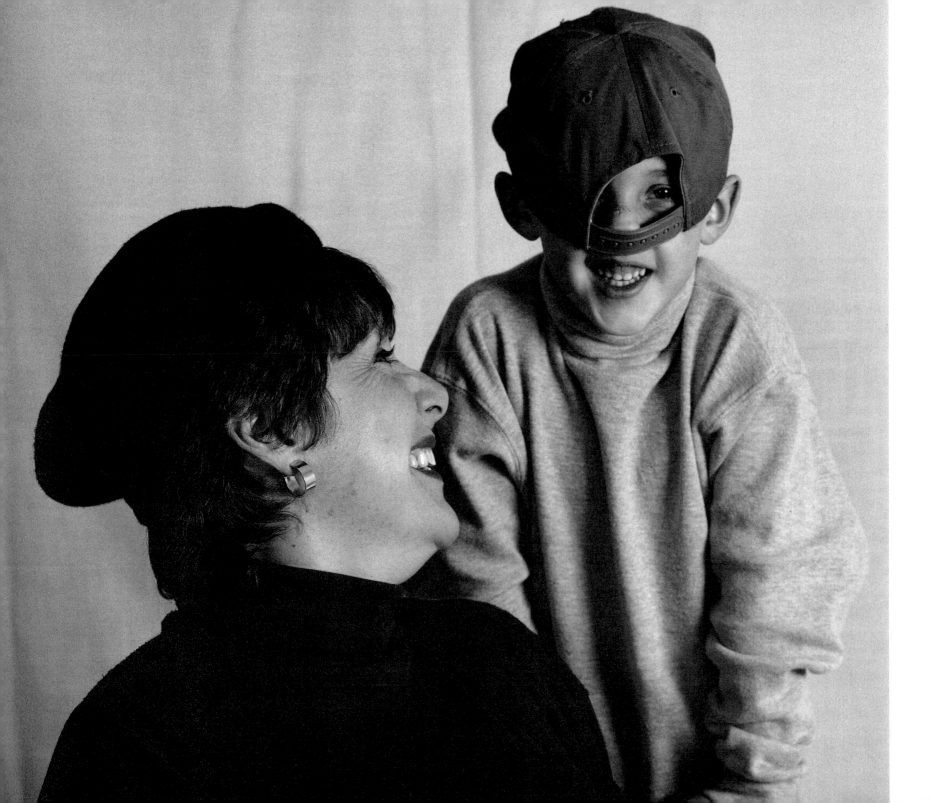

"Who Is My Father?"

SUSAN HOLLANDER

ENGLEWOOD, COLORADO

The catalyst for Susan's deciding to become a single mother was her forty-second birthday. Wanting a biological connection with her child, she decided on donor insemination. Sammy, now six, was born less than a year later. Susan believes that questions about Sammy's biological father will get more complex as he gets older, but she deals with them honestly and openly.

MY SON, SAMMY, had just turned two-and-a-half when a friend first asked him where his father was. This was a situation I had been thinking about ever since I made the decision to be inseminated by donor sperm in 1990. But Sammy, bless his heart, simply said, "Don't have one. You want to play?" The question was really a nonissue for him, and that easy answer sufficed for the moment. This year he started kindergarten, and I know that the questions and answers are going to get more complex as he gets older.

When he was a baby I told Sam about how he came into the world. It was my way of starting to get used to the questions I knew were to come. Sammy knows my simplified version of the way babies are born and that his biological father helps couples and single women who can't have children any other way.

Even though I didn't grow up wanting children, by the time I turned forty I started to think about being a mother. My first and only marriage was a dismal failure, and I knew that I didn't want to have children with my husband. I had always said that if I wasn't pregnant by forty-two, the age my mom was when she had me, I wouldn't have children. Well, when I turned forty-two, I got really depressed. My parents had died several years ago, and when my uncle passed on, I became the last generation. As a biological connection was very important to me, I decided to try and get pregnant. But I didn't know what route to take. Eight years ago there was very little information and no support groups for women who wanted to go the donor-sperm route, and I felt scared and very alone.

It took me almost two years (I'm not exactly a fast mover) to progress from making the decision to become a mother to actually deciding on donor insemination. I met with a specialist in high-risk obstetrics who was very supportive and told me if I wanted to get pregnant I should have done it yesterday. I saw several different infertility specialists before finding one I connected with who would inseminate a single woman. Three months and three inseminations later I was pregnant, at forty-four. As a middle-class, traditional Jewish girl I felt strange, wonderful, and excited all at the same time. But this was not how I had planned to have a family.

When an ultrasound revealed a baby boy, I was thrilled. In retrospect I'm so glad I had a boy, as he has taught me so much about the male side of life—how they feel and think. He has allowed me to experience things that I never have done before.

Chronologically I may be fifty, but I am doing things that most parents do in their thirties, like coaching a beginning soccer team and making mud pies and finger painting. Raising Sammy is my privilege; I can't stress that strongly enough. I can be truly silly with him and let myself go. We laugh a lot and love being together.

When Sammy was born I was both overwhelmed and scared. How would I tell him about how he was born, why I had had him, and where his father is? Would other children make him feel bad and insecure because he doesn't have a father who is truly a father? And would he resent me for making our lives more difficult? The answers to these questions are not easy, but so far, so good. Sammy is a warm and caring little boy who tells me he loves me daily. We have a lot of great male friends who serve as role models and spend time with us. I would love to get married again and have a full-time father for Sammy, but I love my life.

Sammy's questions about his biological father make me think about this wonderful man often. I would love to meet him and thank him for the best gift he could ever have given me—my son.

POSTSCRIPT: Out of her own need, Susan founded the Alliance for Donor Insemination Families in 1995, an organization that gives information and support to prospective parents considering donor insemination, 303-220-8400.

A Deep Capacity for Love

JIM AND JAMIE NESMITH

ALBUQUERQUE, NEW MEXICO

I BELIEVE THAT, in whatever way a three-year-old orphan prays, our Laura Anastasia prayed to God for parents, and the search, the real one, was her search for us rather than the other way around. She needed strong-willed parents with a deep capacity for love. For whatever mysterious reason, God chose us.

There is more to being an adoptive family than retelling the ups and downs that bring them together. When a family opens itself fully to embrace someone beyond its own biology, something else often unfolds: an unexpected reach, a surprising insight, a new view of life.

But God, with His wonderful sense of humor, had one more prayer to answer and decided that this middle-aged couple sitting in a quiet, comfortable home half a world away from Siberia needed a real challenge. Two toddlers! The other prayer came from the heart of a beautiful little boy barely two years old, Joshua Vitaly—a baby born to cuddle and kiss and snuggle, who had a lot of catching up to do in that department.

The very idea of adoption did not cross our minds until we heard of one precious little child whose new family was not working out and for whom there was a chance there would be a disruption. I never saw or held this little life in my arms, but I will hold him in my heart for as long as live. Although he died a tragic

71

death, I honor him in everything I do for my Laura and Joshua.

Three short months after the idea of becoming parents first entered our heads, we were on an airplane headed for Russia. The morning finally arrived when we woke up in Chelyabinsk, Siberia, with the knowledge that it was truly the first day of a new life. I remember how it struck me all at once where we were; I grabbed my husband by the lapels and shouted, "We're in Siberia!" It was quite an event for two people who had grown up in America during the Cold War.

I believed I was prepared for that first meeting. But the reality of actually touching the skin and smelling the sweetness of my two very real children pushed my heart past the boundaries of love previously experienced. My daughter toddled up to me as if there were no one else in the room and held up two tiny fragile arms. I picked up this little feather of a girl, and it was as though three years of longing were wrapped into her grasp.

My baby boy came slowly to my knees, and since I could not take him up, he stood on his tiptoes to get his little head as far into my lap as possible. It was a moment almost too beautiful to bear. The experience of meeting these two felt no different than the enormous love that surged through me at the birth of each of my biological children— deep and strong and forever.

After a few moments I took the reluctant hands of each child and rubbed them against their new daddy's beard. Laura went to him first, and after a while Joshua followed. He has been Daddy's boy ever since.

We spent four hours at that orphanage on the other side of the world. It was clean and neat, and the workers did so much with almost no resources. All the children called us Mama and Papa as they climbed all over us. One little girl, Olga, quietly stayed by Jim the whole time we were there. As we were leaving, the staff was putting the children to bed for their naps. Jim saw Olga lying very still on her cot. Silent tears streaked her face and ran into her dark blonde hair as she stared at the ceiling of her lonely existence. It was a life-changing moment for Jim. The needs of all those children would never be remote and faraway again but always real and urgent. Although we had taken clothes and toys for the orphanage and individual treats for the children who shared a room with ours, coming face to face with the grim reality experienced by so many valuable, precious lives, we knew we had to do more.

Back home in Albuquerque we were coping, in survival mode. Institutionalized children have been described as "not normal" kids. I disagree. They are normal kids who have survived very difficult circumstances by learning coping techniques that served them well in that environment. It takes work and patience and unconditional love to replace survival skills with socially acceptable skills.

Two things kept us going: the enormous love and respect Jim and I have for each other, and our very special family.

We had arrived home, bone weary, to an immaculately clean house compliments of our older children, Chris and Amy, and Chris's wife, Leslie. As a welcome home gift to their new sister and brother, they had transformed the children's room into a storybook land of Winnie the Pooh. Chris and Leslie, in their mid twenties and with careers of their own, moved in for nine months to help us through the adjustment. In every free moment they cleaned, ran errands, shopped for us, prepared meals, and chased, bathed, rescued, comforted, played with, and loved Laura and Joshua.

Amy, a busy college student, came over frequently to play and cuddle and to take mountains of pictures. More than once she has done our laundry or cleaned the kitchen. She even kept a personal crisis in her own life to herself for many months to protect us from additional stress.

Chris and Amy, born during my first marriage, were my teachers in the ancient art of parenthood. Although they happened to have been born of my body, they came *through* me, not *from* me. I came to understand that I am not a creator of life but rather a privileged gardener chosen to nurture what God has created. They already were who they were meant to be when they were born and could not be transformed and molded according to my expecta-

tions. As I watched these young adults pour their generous hearts into loving acts for Joshua and Laura, I was so very thankful I had not ruined my beautiful wild rose and snapdragon by trying to turn them into orchids. And I look forward, once again, to watching two more precious lives bloom into their own unique beauty.

Additionally, Jim's brother, Frank, his wife, Mardi, and his daughter, Kelee, made two oak rocking horses, painted, signed, and dated, for the children, which were strong and beautiful with the hours of love that went into them. They will be heirlooms for Joshua and Laura to pass down as they tell future generations our family's story of love.

My parents, now eighty-eight and seventy-nine years old, took these children into their hearts just like the eight grandchildren who had come before them. My dad marvels at their strength and courage, and in special moments my mom reaches out and takes one of them in her arms and, with tears in her eyes, thanks God that they are safe with us.

There have been rough places in the road as well. Both Laura and Joshua have medical problems that may affect them the rest of their lives. We discovered these when they had been home for about three months. The tragedy is that they would have been completely avoidable with proper medical care and supplies. We were again reminded of the tremendous shortages and challenges in the children's hospitals and orphanages in the former Soviet

Union. They had given us so much. We needed to do something, but what?

I had the desire, but for Jim it was a burning quest—maybe even his destiny. He had embraced the challenge of parenting my older children as teenagers and had adjusted his intellectual mind to making a comfortable place in his life for little Laura and Joshua. Jim Nesmith was already my knight in shining armor; however, there was still more to this wonderful man than even I knew. Within six months of bringing our children home, on top of his already overwhelming responsibilities, he carved out the time and energy to create an organization to repay Russia for the privilege of parenting two beautiful children.

Working at Los Alamos Labs with Jim are Carol Wilkinson and her husband, Vern Sandberg, who adopted a two-year-old girl from Chelyabinsk, and Ken Bower and his wife, who adopted four children domestically. They talked about the serious conditions in the children's hospitals and orphanages in Russia. Jim, Carol, and Vern had all witnessed firsthand the conditions under which very capable, compassionate, and caring people were fighting daily on behalf of these children

As the group talked and planned, they chose the name *Yabloka,* or "apple" in Russian, for their organization, because it is a universally recognized symbol of good health and nutrition. At that moment the Yabloka Children's Fund was born.

Jim and I know that our job is to honor, admire, and celebrate the individual value of every child and to expand that view to help children who are "ours" in a different sense—those whom we will never hold or caress or tuck into bed at night. After all, God creates all children. Each one is a precious, valuable life. We know we can't save them all, but that does not relieve us of the responsibility of giving our best to repay God for the unspeakable joy and privilege of parenting the four He has entrusted to our care.

NOTE: The Yabloka Children's Fund is a nonprofit corporation dedicated to providing medicine, medical supplies, and developmental materials to orphanages and children's hospitals throughout Russia. The fund is currently providing desperately needed items to a variety of children's institutions in Russia. All items are personally delivered to ensure that they arrive safely at their intended destination. For more information about the Yabloka Children's Fund write to 2861 Trevino Drive, Rio Rancho, NM 87124, or explore the organization's Web site at www.yabloka.org.

Fulfilling Their Destiny

LeVar and Stephanie Burton

Sherman Oaks, California

Although a medical condition meant Stephanie would not be able to conceive without doctors' intervention, the most significant barrier to parenthood for the Burtons was LeVar's unresolved emotional issues about becoming a father again. Once he crossed that psychic bridge, however, he never looked back, and the couple's path to parenthood unfolded with few obstacles.

LEVAR: The story of our family really revolves, as it should, around the deep love that Stephanie and I have for each other. When I first met Stephanie ten years ago, I knew she was my life partner. I also knew that, with all her being, she wanted to be a mother. Truthfully, I felt torn by this longing and my own uncertainty about whether to become a father again. I already had a son, Eian, who was then seven years old and is a large part of my life. But my intense love for this woman and the recognition of her intense desire to have a child made my decision an easy one in the end, and one I've never regretted.

STEPHANIE: I have always known that I was put on this planet to be a mother. I love that role—it is what I do best—but it requires time and the commitment to really being available to your child to do the job well. For a long time children didn't figure in my plans. As I approached forty, I knew that my mind was ready but my body was going to give me trouble. I was eager to start looking at our options, but my gynecologist told me, "Relax, go home, and have unprotected sex for six months." I fired him on the spot—we'd been having unprotected sex for seven years! I felt certain that in vitro fertilization was my best option, but LeVar wasn't fully committed to the idea of becoming a father quite yet. We decided to harvest and save my eggs while he worked to resolve the issue to his satisfaction, but shortly before I went in for the retrieval we decided to try a cycle. Soon after I was implanted with four of my fertilized eggs, and two weeks later I was pregnant.

LEVAR: The moment Stephanie told me that God was telling her it was time to try to conceive, I had to listen to her. She has this wonderful spiritual quality, and we've learned to listen to and trust her inner voices. The disconcerting awkwardness of having to ejaculate into a paper cup, and the fear and implications of what this said about my manhood, quickly became insignificant when I saw how much this meant to her. Stephanie's most fervent fear—of needles—came up against her most fervent desire as she injected herself with hormones every day for thirty days. Watching her struggle to overcome this fear, I vowed to do whatever it took to give Stephanie the baby she dreamed of night and day.

Although I realize we were incredibly lucky, it came as no surprise to me that we beat the odds and became pregnant the first time. I remember that day vividly, because we experienced the highest high and lowest low we had ever had together in one fifteen-minute period. Stephanie had taken a pregnancy test at our doctor's office, and then took another one at home that came back negative. She was devastated. She needed some time to be alone, so I went out to work in the office, when the phone rang. "You two are going to be such great parents," Kathy, our fertility nurse told me. Apparently our home pregnancy test had been wrong, and now I got to deliver the fabulous news to Stephanie.

STEPHANIE: I was ready to be pregnant and wanted to experience the whole process to the fullest. I had started on a pregnancy-specific physical fitness and nutrition program and did everything possible to create the best possible conditions for the baby growing inside me. I was delighted to be having a little girl, and Michaela turned out to be exactly what I prayed for.

By choice I had put my career on hold to become a full-time mother, but I found that I missed being in a professional environment. As wonderful as full-time motherhood was, I knew that returning part-time to the workplace would provide a balance in my life that would broaden my perspective and make me a better mother. When Michaela was eighteen months old I went back to work two days a week doing the other thing I love to do, being a makeup artist. I now have the best of both worlds. I was home to experience the magical baby and toddler years and to give my daughter the kind of attention every child deserves. Even now, with Michaela in preschool, I love planning for our adventures and other outings. I care about my career, but my daughter will always come first. Cutting back on my lifestyle and spending more time at home is a worthwhile trade-off to achieve the perfect balance between meeting her needs and mine.

LEVAR: The best thing about being a parent is children, and the worst thing about being a parent is children. Michaela's arrival in our lives was only the first of many surprises I could never have predicted ten years ago. I truly believe that I have a destiny to fulfill and a path to travel that includes my work and my family. Being a father as I move along this spiritual path has made me realize that we only reach this destination by focusing on the journey. I try to maintain this focus to create a comfortable environment while I'm at work on a movie or television set as well as in my home. How we treat each other in our daily lives and communicate with each other is an important part of the journey, so I listen to my children, to really hear what they are telling me. Our lives are about being in the moment and making every day and every encounter

meaningful—and then being able to let go. I love being a father. It is far, far more fulfilling than I ever imagined it to be. Michaela and Stephanie make it so.

STEPHANIE: Having Michaela and LeVar makes my team complete for this mission called life. I have a focus and purpose now that was never quite so clarified before. I am content with my roles as mother and wife, and with that part of my life completely fulfilled, it frees me up to go out into the world to meet and conquer my challenges. I am Mommy—hear me roar!

A "Small Happiness"

MARTHA GROVES

LOS ANGELES, CALIFORNIA

"If I can survive this, I can raise a child on my own," reasoned Martha Groves, a business reporter for the Los Angeles Times. *As a cancer survivor she had reason for concern as she set out on a soul-searching two-week camping trip, a self-imposed test of endurance to see if she had both the stamina and the integrity to be a single mother. Evidently she did, and in June 1994 she left for China to bring home her then fifteen-month-old daughter, Nora Tai-Xiu.*

WHENEVER STRANGERS ASK how long it took me to adopt my delightful daughter, Nora Tai-Xiu, from China, I reply, "Seven months. Shorter than a pregnancy." But the real answer is more like ten years and seven months. Ten years to muster up the courage to be a single mother, and seven months to go hell-bent on making the adoption happen.

In late 1983 I was diagnosed with cervical cancer. Having just turned thirty-three and being determined to preserve my ability to conceive and carry a child, over the next two years I endured five surgeries, including a radiation implant that required me to lie in a drug-induced stupor for most of a week. Without getting into the gory medical details, suffice it to say that the experience was an emotionally grueling roller-coaster ride that plunged me repeatedly from soaring hope to crushing despair. The disease won out, and at thirty-six I had a hysterectomy.

Friends kept telling me how lucky I was to be alive. Instead I felt cheated

and morbidly depressed, because I urgently craved a child to love and nurture. "Go to church," my mother in Indiana advised. "You'll feel better." But I would sit sniffling in my pew, constantly reminded by all the infants and toddlers around me of what I did not have.

A string of ill-fated romances didn't help. I increasingly found that the men I met would make the sign of the cross—as in "Go away, Dracula"— whenever I brought up the adoption issue. Since I had bought into the old-fashioned notion that securing a husband is a prerequisite to parenthood, my situation seemed hopeless.

In the spring of 1993, while a San Francisco correspondent for the *Los Angeles Times,* I read a local newspaper story about overseas adoption, focusing on China. I had already heard tales about baby girls being abandoned—or worse—because the nation's age-old cultural preference for boys had collided with its one-child-per-family rule imposed to control the burgeoning population.

Something clicked. Given how unfathomable I found the opposite sex to be, I realized that I definitely wanted to adopt a girl. Moreover, domestic adoptions were problematic for forty-something, single women like me, and in California they were further complicated by laws giving biological parents six months to reclaim a child.

In China, meanwhile, tens of thousands of unwanted infant and toddler girls were languishing in orphanages. The fact that I was older and single would not be an impediment there. China required that would-be parents be at least thirty-five, and single women were welcomed.

With hope tempered by trepidation I attended an informational meeting sponsored by a Bay Area adoption agency. After listening to tales of parents who had brought back bundles of joy from South America and Hong Kong, I was tempted, yet I concluded that the whole thing was just too daunting—and outside my grasp financially.

A few months later, after one last dating fiasco, I rented a Ford Explorer and began a twelve-day camping trek. My three-thousand-mile solo jaunt took me from the parched canyon lands of Utah, where the desert heat popped the corks on the bottles of merlot I was hauling, to the deep-freeze country of Wyoming's Grand Tetons, where I scraped ice crystals off my tent fly in the morning. As I shlepped the cooler and pitched my tent and shopped for ice and chopped wood and dodged moose and bears on miles of hiking trails, I regretted not building in any time to just cogitate. "You're not processing," I chided myself.

On my last night out I bunked at a coworker's home in northern California. Freed of my camping chores, I could finally relax a bit. By morning I sensed a transformation. Instead of feeling insecure and frightened at the prospect of being a mom, suddenly I felt as capable as Superwoman. Surviving my camping trip had given me a big dose of confidence. As I pulled out of the driveway in the morning I told my friend that I had reached two decisions: I was giving up on dating, and I was going to adopt a baby girl from China.

As I had learned from my cancer experience, wanting something really badly does not make it so. Early in 1993 China imposed a moratorium on adoptions so that it could get its bureaucratic house in order. By fall it was still in place. Nonetheless, my adoption agency urged me to start the paperwork, which filled a binder four inches thick. Over the next few weeks I set up three sessions with a county social worker chosen to determine my parent-worthiness and to compose my "home study," a ubiquitous requirement that summarizes one's background and circumstances.

I began immersing myself in the Chinese culture—not a difficult endeavor in San Francisco. I took walking and culinary tours in Chinatown and devoured books by Chinese authors. References to the Asian bias in favor of boys were routine. "Slave," I learned, is one meaning of a Chinese word for "female." A newborn girl in China is considered to be a "small happiness," whereas a baby boy is a "big happiness."

By year's end my agency was spreading the good word that China was once again open for adoptions. In March 1994 I contacted Charles Chen, an ambitious Chinese entrepreneur in the commercial center of Shenzhen, across the border from Hong Kong. He had helped find children for other of my agency's clients and vowed to locate a healthy infant girl for me.

Buoyed by his optimism, I prepared a set of documents for the Chinese authorities. Then, in April, Charles broke the news that the rules had changed. Beijing was taking charge of identifying children for prospective parents. He also mentioned that there were two hundred applications ahead of mine and that I should brace myself for a long wait.

On the morning of May 25 I got an unexpected call from my agency. "Beijing has assigned you a baby girl!" the woman said. Her name was Tai-Xiu (pronounced more or less like "tie shoe"), and she lived at the social welfare institution in Taizhou, a city northwest of Shanghai in Jiangsu Province. I could pick her up in June.

I began literally to quiver with joy. But I sensed hesitation in the woman's voice. "What's the problem?" I asked. "Is she healthy?" "Yes, but she's older than you wanted. She was born March 18, 1993." Calculating quickly, I realized that she would be fifteen months old when I met her.

I burst into tears, feeling thwarted yet again in my desire to mother a tiny, helpless infant. The woman needed an answer within four hours. This was my one shot, she cautioned, because the agency was reluctant to rock the boat. If I said no, I could forget about adopting from China.

face perched over a puffy yellow-and-white snowsuit and topped by a pink snow hat. I had color blowups made and put them up all around my apartment.

A month of nearly sleepless nights later I left with my mother, Faye, for China, where we hooked up with a group of other prospective parents from the Bay Area. When we reached hot, muggy Nanjing, Charles, the facilitator, introduced us to the orphanage director. He handed me an updated photo of Tai-Xiu, showing a bewildered-looking toddler with a heart-melting half-moon frown.

After lunch the next day and meetings with various Chinese bureaucrats, we settled into our hotel room for what we presumed would be several hours of waiting. But within minutes, hearing a commotion in the hallway, I peered out on a scene of sheer pandemonium. With no fanfare, the orphanage nurses had arrived and were parceling out a gaggle of babies, most of them in tears.

Tai-Xiu, the second oldest of the group, was clearly aware that some dramatic change was happening and wanted nothing to do with me, this blond, blue-eyed "new mama," as the nurses identified me. When the orphanage director tried to hand her over, she straightened out like a board. I backed away, hurt but aware that this was an appropriate reaction, given her discombobulation. Finally the nurses motioned to me to take her. As Tai-Xiu sobbed, I tenderly stroked her hair and, heart bursting, fell madly and instantly in love.

After quick consultations with friends and family (initially skeptical and unsupportive, my parents had by this time embraced my desire to adopt), I decided to go for it. In some cosmic sense I felt that this was the child for me and that I would feel disloyal if I rejected her. The next day brought a photo the size of a postage stamp. It showed a tiny, adorable moon

84

I wept along with her, tears of joy and relief and gratitude. After seven months—and ten years—I was at last a mother. Over games played with Cheerios and take-out dinners of rice and steamed dumplings, Nora (named for my late grandmother) and I took to each other. She was soon calling me "Mama," and far from being sad, she emerged as a cheerful, impish, affectionate tyke.

Near the end of our stay in China, as I toted my nineteen-pound cherub in a backpack through a hotel shop, a Chinese woman stopped to thank me in broken English for adopting a little girl. "She is lucky baby," she said. "Oh, no," I hastened to assure her tearfully, "I am the lucky one." And, indeed, there is no doubt in my mind that it was Nora who did the rescuing, not the other way around.

I often wonder about her unknown birth mother and what the circumstances were that drove her to abandon her baby girl. As Nora continues to blossom into a bright and charming little girl, I wish I could tell my counterpart in China how well we're doing—and thank her for making my world complete. By relinquishing her "small happiness," she gave me the greatest gift that life could ever bring.

The Lost Boys

Eric and Greg Wolfson-Sagot

Los Angeles, California

GREG: We talked about children on our first date, and Eric convinced me that adoption was the best way to go. Two years later we went through a foster parent orientation and we knew that this would be our path; that we could do something so necessary as well as fulfilling our dream. We found the Los Angeles County Department of Children and Family Services to be very open toward gay and lesbian foster parents. Christopher was our first placement, in the fall of 1994. I was twenty-nine and Eric was twenty-four. At that time we were the youngest foster parents the agency ever had. Little did we know how unusual our family was in the outside world.

ERIC: We decided to become foster parents even if it meant we wouldn't be able to keep the child we were parenting forever. But when we met Christopher it was an immediate match. By the time he was fifteen months old he had been

When Greg and Eric decided to be parents, they chose to adopt through the Los Angeles County Foster system. Christopher came to them at fifteen months old in October of 1994 and his adoption was final in June of 1996. In late 1996, Sammy was presented to them at fourteen months old, and his adoption was finalized in January 1998. Both Eric and Greg feel strongly about adoption as an alternative method of becoming a family and found being foster parents a rewarding experience.

have to be very clever and persistent to adopt through the foster care system. Copies of our paperwork were lost and phone calls to social workers were not returned for weeks, as their workload is so tremendous. But these are the children who need our love and help.

We reorganized our priorities completely to have this baby. Greg took time off work and stayed home for nearly a year to give Chris the cohesive and loving second year that he so desperately needed. We lost contact with most of our friends and became best friends with each other.

GREG: The first year was very lonely. After losing my career identity, it was difficult to find friends. Most people in our circle were uncomfortable with us now that we were parents, and the parents in our neighborhood were older professionals with full-time nannies and on a very different path than we were.

We found the gay community, while seemingly fascinated with us, pretty unaccommodating of our situation (complaining in restaurants if the kids made any noise, jealous of the attention that we needed to give to our child even if they were in the middle of a story). Finally after more than eighteen months, we met Steven, George, and Katie, a male couple with a two-year-old girl, and Karen, Kathy, and Ben, a female couple with a three-year-old boy, who also felt adrift from the

unable to bond with any of the foster parents. He bonded with us on the night we met. We began a five-week process of completing our foster license before we could take him home, so we ended up commuting two hours a day to visit him in his foster home. From there we began the long and arduous process of making our situation permanent. You

community. Slowly we have met more and more gay and lesbian families.

Eric and I are both up front about our family. Our kids' schools know the score and so do their doctors and their friends' parents. In public, however, we frequently have to "come out" a lot. People often say, "Where's Mommy today?" and we always answer that they have two dads.

I went back to work after Chris turned two and started pre-school. I am fortunate enough to have an incredibly flexible schedule, so that when Chris was three and his adoption was final we decided to become parents again. We debated whether or not to put up with the hassles of fostering (paperwork, visits from social workers) and decided that the positive outweighed the negative. In November of 1996 we were matched with fourteen-month-old Sammy and were overjoyed. After the first few hours we realized that something wasn't right with him, and took him to the doctor. He had pneumonia and severe diaper rash, both due to neglect. We found out that he also suffered from sensory integration dysfunction which caused many problems for him, including the inability to feel pain, lack of balance, frenetic energy, boundless anger and frustration, and the fear of sleep. His only method of communication was an ear-piercing shriek.

We had a long struggle with finding a diagnosis for him, then finding therapies, and finding the funding for these therapies and the effects they had on our ability to support ourselves.

Fortunately, after battling for the services Sammy needed, he received speech therapy twice a week, occupational therapy twice a week, and five days a week in an intensive infant special needs program. Things are turning around for him and he is improving rapidly.

ERIC: Although Sammy's unique needs have been difficult, we have never regretted adopting him or becoming foster parents. This type of parenting allows you to truly make a difference in a child's life. What you need to be a foster parent is a loving home. In our county, foster children have only a seven percent chance of being adopted, so a consistent and loving person in these children's lives is so much better than what they had. Social workers know that good homes for children exist with single people, gays, and lesbians of all income levels and races.

As our boys continue to grow, we will have to face many unique challenges. Christopher is already wondering where his birth mother is and why he has two daddies. We explain that his birth mother was too sick to take care of him, and because he was involved with Sam's adoption, he thinks that babies come from foster families. Our definition of a family has changed dramatically since we became parents. Before having children we cared about each other, our friends, and our house. Now we have this wonderful family and it comes first for both of us, and we take care of it and nurture it.

Kudos to the Coach!

CATHY GUISEWITE

STUDIO CITY, CALIFORNIA

O N MY THIRTY-NINTH BIRTHDAY I gave myself the ultimatum: I had one year to get into a relationship that had a chance of leading to marriage and motherhood. On my fortieth birthday I gave myself a one-year extension. When I turned forty-one and was no closer to even having a good first date, I decided it was time to really consider other options. At that point I honestly didn't know if I ever really wanted to be married, but I was absolutely sure I wanted to be a mother. I knew a few couples who had adopted children, and I called them for the names of the attorneys they'd used.

Cartoonist Cathy Guisewite has experienced more than two decades of success with her "Cathy" comic strip. But when she decided at age forty-one that she wanted to adopt a baby as a single mother, she was stunned by the roadblocks she encountered. Cathy never would have persevered if she hadn't found Nikki, an adoption facilitator who gave her the confidence and support she needed to see it through. She has been there for Cathy and her daughter, Ivy, now five, ever since.

It's one thing to think about adoption and quite a different thing to make the phone call that could lead to a little soul being placed in your arms for the rest of your life. I finally called the offices of four adoption attorneys, and I remember feeling so insecure that the questions I was asking on the phone were all but drowned out by the questions I was asking myself in my mind: "What are

you doing?" "You've failed at relationships for forty-one years; what makes you think you can be someone's mother?" "How on earth are you going to work a baby into your schedule?" "Is it right to bring a baby into a family without a father?" "If you really, really try, don't you think you could meet someone, fall in love, get married, and get pregnant in the next six months?"

The first three calls were very short. I heard just enough to have my insecurities slightly rein-

forced, and I got off the phone. When I called the last number on my list an adoption facilitator named Nikki Biers answered the phone. She had the most amazing, reassuring way about her that not only made me feel it was absolutely possible for me to adopt a baby but also that the anxieties I had about doing it were all pretty valid and were things she could help me look at. Our first phone call lasted about half an hour and resembled a miniature therapy session. I went to meet Nikki in person a few days later, talked a lot more, found out specifics on how adoption works, and then spent a few more months really thinking about whether I was ready to have her try to help me create a family.

Every adoptive parent I know feels the child they have was meant to be with them as surely as if they'd given birth to him or her—that some divine force guided them to this child because they were meant to be together. In my case, I think God created my daughter for me and then realized He needed Nikki to nudge me into position.

Nikki called me several times during my "contemplation months" just to see how I was doing and to remind me she was there if I wanted to talk to someone about my decision-making process. What Nikki did best was to help me sort out what was just blind fear of the unknown and what was a real issue that I should try to deal with before moving forward. Maybe most important, she helped me keep my sense of humor the whole time.

My parents were completely supportive of the idea of my adopting a child, but asking a prospective grandma or grandpa (especially one who had been waiting for forty-one years) for a calm discussion of the pros and cons wasn't exactly realistic. In many ways I think Nikki helped me have all the conversations a married person contemplating adoption has with his or her spouse. Nikki referred to it as "going in baby steps:" I needed to just take one small step at a time, to stop the process when it didn't feel right and to go forward when it did.

Then one day Nikki called to tell me she had someone she wanted me to meet. I can only equate it to being asked to go on the blind date of my life. Nothing in life can prepare a woman for the moment when she meets the mother of her child. In retrospect, I think what carried both my daughter's birth mother and me through that day was that, on the deepest possible level, we both knew that we had each just found the most important person in our life—someone who, in a nanosecond, had gone from being a complete stranger to the person with whom we would have the most profound connection we would ever know.

Nikki was there in every way for both the birth mother and me through the rest of the pregnancy. She came to the hospital as soon as Ivy was born and took the picture that's among my most treasured things: of Ivy being held between both of the mothers who love her so much.

My daughter has changed my life, improved my life, refocused my life, redefined every relationship in my life, and expanded my universe a million times over. She has both forced me to be a grown-up and given me the chance to be a little girl again.

Nikki, her husband, and her children have since become wonderful, close friends. Ivy and I get together with them often, and I'm their youngest daughter's godmother. I never see Nikki without reliving the day I called her office and being astounded all over again by the miracle that grew from my first conversation with her. It was, for me, my daughter's moment of conception. Last year, Nikki went on to found her own agency, The Adoption Circle.

I have had a very blessed life in many ways, but without Nikki I wouldn't be the person I'm the most proud of being—Ivy's mother.

POSTSCRIPT: Cathy recently got married to Chris Wilkison, the father of a young son, Cooper. They have created a blended family, and when Cooper gets a little bit older he will live with Cathy, Ivy, and his father on a half-time basis. "Ivy is excited about having a little brother but not very happy about sharing the attention and her toys," says Cathy. "This family is now a work in progress, with lots of changes and new experiences."

The phone number for The Adoption Circle is (818) 762–9839.

Part III

In the Parenting Trenches

···

MOST OF US RECOGNIZE A STRONG, effective family when we see one. Its members are committed and connected to one another and seem to take in stride whatever life metes out. They are, in a word, *resilient*. Resilient families embody a sense of tradition and a spirit of flexibility in the way they function. In other words, they have a way to stand and a way to bend. This is essential for healthy growth.

The image of parents "in the trenches" suggests that there is a lot going on in families during the years just before and during adolescence. It takes real commitment for parents to dig in for the long haul and continue working to build a stable, secure place where all family members are affirmed, supported, respected, trusted, and heard despite occasional skirmishes, surprise attacks, ground fire, and temporary sellouts to the enemy. A capacity for optimism, resourcefulness, and perseverance is at the heart of families who work together for positive growth.

Sooner or later most nontraditional families find themselves facing the outside world's perception that *different* means *inferior* or something less than the current norm. The way a family chooses to acknowledge and validate questions and feelings about how they came together—whether through adoption, surrogacy, remarriage, or any of the infinite combinations that can make a family—speaks to their own feelings about difference. How parents convey their own acceptance and understanding to their children is just one more parenting task added to the package.

Clearly these families are comfortable with the choices they have made and have communicated that attitude to their kids. Their stories illustrate how a family's approach to work and play, rituals and traditions, shared responsibility, respect for individual differences, and service to others beyond one's own immediate circle strengthens and deepens the family connection. These stories honor individual differences and contributions; illustrate how lives have moved in new, sometimes unexpected directions; and reveal the unconditional love, acceptance, and joy that evolves from living each day in a family.

Naomi's Story: A Tale of Commitment

JOSHUA AND FROMA FALLIK

PHOENIX, ARIZONA

A BAR OR BAT MITZVAH is a celebration of a child's taking his or her place as an adult in the Jewish community. For adopted children it is the time when they, rather than their parents, get to decide whether or not they want to embrace the Jewish faith and live fully as a Jew. At Naomi's Bat Mitzvah in 1991 she said, "In the portion of the Bible that we read this week, the children of Israel are on the verge of beginning a new life, leaving Egypt on their way to Mt. Sinai and the land of Israel. Like them, I, too, started a new life. Four years ago, I left the country where I was born. It was very hard.

Strong, resilient families embody a sense of tradition and a spirit of flexibility in the way they function. When parents choose to adopt an older child, they must be open and willing to accept that child for the person he or she is and set aside any notions about how the child "should" be. Naomi was adopted from Korea by an Orthodox Jewish family when she was eight years old. Hers is a story with multicultural dimensions. It illustrates her family's acceptance, unconditional support, and commitment to her as she was coming to terms with her own emerging identity.

"We are taught that a person who converts undergoes all the same experiences as the children of Israel did at Mt. Sinai. So today, by agreeing to observe the mitzvoth [commandments], I complete my own personal Sinai. Although I

Korea and joined Jed, five, and Rachel, one, as our oldest. She seemed so fragile, but she was, and still is, an incredibly strong person. Within three months of her arrival Naomi let us know that she wanted to attend Yeshiva, a Hebrew day school, just like her new brother. We had planned to wait at least a year before raising the question of a dual language (Hebrew and English) program, believing Naomi would not be comfortable in one until she was familiar with at least one of the languages. But Naomi knew what she wanted to do, and so, overcoming our great concern, we enrolled her in Yeshiva, where she thrived.

Almost four years later, our twelve-year-old daughter was to decide for herself if she really wanted to live her life as a Jew. Naomi knew that the decisions we had made for her would not bind her unless she chose this path for herself as an adult. She knew that as a non-Jew she would only have to obey the Ten Laws of Noah, laws like not committing murder and living in a lawful society, to be considered a good person. As a Jew, however, she would pledge to observe 613 commandments, including the laws concerning food and the Sabbath. As a child who had spent the last four years in an Orthodox Jewish household, she knew this was no small decision.

After several months of thought, Naomi decided to proceed. How would we celebrate? My husband and I had our own ideas, but what we

won't be faced with forty years of wandering in the desert, I know that there are still obstacles that I will have to overcome."

We adopted Naomi when she was already eight and a half years old. She came to us from

wanted was irrelevant. Naomi knew exactly what she wanted, to prepare a scholarly dissertation on the portion of the Torah that we would read that week, and to present it surrounded by the people she loved.

We wondered if she could really handle the research. Even if she could, would she be able to write the paper? And then, could my shy and retiring daughter really speak before the two hundred friends and relatives on our pared-down list of guests? Could I cook for two hundred people? Would all of them fit into our house, even if we removed most of the furniture? The answers, thankfully, turned out to be yes, yes, yes, yes, and yes again!

Naomi labored endlessly over that speech. She chose a great Torah portion, beginning with the midwives thwarting Pharaoh's order to kill the Jewish babies. The story moved through the adoption of baby Moses by Pharaoh's daughter, Basya, and concludes with Moses's wife, Tzipporah, fighting with an angel to save her husband's life. Naomi wrote, "These women all have one thing in common. They all stood up for what they knew was right, no matter who they had to confront; their father, their king, even an angel. And they have another thing in common, too. According to Jewish tradition, they are all converts."

After studying the Torah portion, Naomi reviewed the classic commentaries of Rashi and Abravenel. Then she read the legends and stories associated with her portion, and finally she studied Nechama Leibowitz, one of the great modern commentators. She discussed the themes she wanted to emphasize and took copious notes. And then she began to write.

Naomi's speech was incredibly polished. Naomi herself looked poised, beautiful, and so mature. And surrounded by people who loved her, people who remembered a skinny, scared little girl who didn't speak a word of English and hid in a corner when friends came to meet her, she didn't leave a dry eye in the house.

Naomi concluded by saying, "Even after the children of Israel received the Torah at Mt. Sinai, they still had a long journey before they could enter the land of Israel, the Promised Land. I, too, still have a long journey of learning the Torah and keeping mitzvoth ahead of me. I know that Torah learning is never ending. I know that this is just a beginning."

POSTSCRIPT: Naomi kept her word and is actively living out the commitment made at her Bat Mitzvah six years ago. She has just completed a year of studies at a university in Israel and is currently attending university and living in New York City.

Parenting Challenging Children: A Survival Guide for Happy Endings

TORIN SCOTT, CONFIDENTIAL INTERMEDIARY

SCOTTSDALE, ARIZONA

Torin Scott, a single mom, has been an adoption advocate and foster parent since her twenties. Today she is the adoptive mom of two sibling groups, totaling five children, all with severe emotional and attention deficits. The entire family was honored at the White House during National Adoption Month in 1997. When the funding for their trip fell through at the last moment, they were rescued by none other than Dave Thomas, himself a strong advocate of adoption, who was also in town to be honored. And where did they go for supper? Why, Wendy's, of course!

*I*N THE FIFTEEN YEARS that I have been involved in adoption, I have watched in sadness as the families of some of my friends have fallen apart under the stress of parenting their adopted children, especially those with special needs. Left with little more than battle scars and a deep, empty ache, these adoptive parents often feel victimized, guilty, and isolated. Instead of words of support from their friends, they have often endured references to "bad blood" and remarks such as, "What did you expect? Did you think you were Wonder Woman or Superman?"

Any adult choosing adoption today must be prepared to accept a child—whether an infant or an older child at time of placement—for who the child is,

enough. It takes commitment, endurance, and acceptance.

Not every child will be able to return your love or show it in the way you expect. It is important, therefore, to get your own needs met elsewhere. Your son or daughter did not agree to adopt you; it was *your* plan. It is not fair to blame him if he doesn't agree with it. Take responsibility for your plan, and remember that you can't fix everything. Neither can anyone else. Refuse to accept blame for things that are beyond your control.

Parents of children with special challenges must learn to savor the good moments as they appear. The good times with your child may not always equal the difficult ones. Enjoy each precious moment, and hold it in your heart to draw on when things are rough. Don't spoil the good times by harboring grudges or maintaining an emotional distance. Have a sense of humor, and learn to step back from a bad situation. It will help keep things in perspective.

Whether parenting alone or as a couple, it is critical that you identify and build a strong support system for yourself. There will be times when you need to vent your frustration or cry on a shoulder, and you need to have a healthy adult on the receiving end. Don't expect neighbors, family, friends, or even a therapist to always understand your adoption decisions. They can't. They haven't lived them. Don't blame them for their lack of understanding; just

not for the person she might have been had she been born into a stable family who loved her from day one. Abuse and neglect before and after birth exact a huge toll. It is important to grieve over who the child might have been, and then let it go. Love unconditionally. Love fiercely. Love enough for the both of you, and realize that love alone is not

accept that you have developed some expertise in an area that they have not.

While you're building outside support, it is equally important to take care of yourself by keeping both physically and mentally healthy. It is the best gift you can give yourself as you face each new day. And don't overlook others in the family who are doing well. They can be your reservoir of joy and laughter. Too often the noisy or difficult child grabs most of your time and attention, but the others have needs that must be honored and met without their having to act out to be noticed.

As you move through each day, use your knowledge, your anger, your joy, and your frustration and direct it where it will do some good. Advocate not only for your child but also for others who cannot speak for themselves. Lobby or write. Speak out and get involved. This will also provide you with a healthy outlet. The parenting years are a good time to renew and share your faith, however you define it. If you believe you are not alone and that things happen for a reason, even though we may not understand it at the time, it will give you strength.

In the final analysis, there are no pat or easy answers to parenting adopted kids. Each family must decide on its own course when things are not going according to the plans they made or the dreams they dreamed. I have grown and matured in ways I could not have imagined when I began this journey. I have learned much about love and acceptance. I have learned about strength and commitment. And I have come to understand and respect my children's challenges and needs. Although parenting them sometimes feels like putting Band-Aids on broken bones, it is not a fruitless endeavor. Adoption is changing the world one dirty sock at a time, and adopting attachment-disordered or emotionally challenged children is mending a broken heart one tantrum at a time. Although it may not show for years, I believe each tantrum that ends with your child being rocked in your arms puts a tiny glimmer back into his heart. That glimmer is hope. And it is the presence or absence of hope that makes or breaks a family.

An Unexpected Blessing

Tom and Joanne Ashe

Placitas, New Mexico

The adoption of Tolya, now ten, changed the lives of Tom and Joanne Ashe in unexpected ways. Most recently, they have completed a half-hour-long documentary on the lives and thoughts of orphanage children in Russia, with Tolya himself interpreting the poignant longings expressed by children whose existence he understands so well.

WHY WOULD A FAMILY that appeared to have a perfect life suddenly risk that balance? This was the question our friends and relatives asked when they heard that we were about to adopt our Russian son, Anatoly.

My preoccupation with orphans began when I was a young girl, the middle child of two Holocaust survivors. My parents lost everyone to the ravages of the Holocaust—their parents, grandparents, siblings, aunts, uncles, cousins . . . seventy-six in all. They met just two days after my father walked out of the Mauthausen concentration camp as a free man. My mother had survived by assuming a false identity as a Christian. All alone in the world, they had no choice but to manage their own lives as best they could.

Growing up I could sense the deep pain running through the hearts of my beloved parents. I felt our loneliness in the world. I would often daydream about children separated from their parents, lost in the world. My spirit reached out to

other Americans, viewed the program *20/20* and was shocked by footage of the Romanian orphans born and abandoned in their country under the reign of Ceausescu. My smug complacency was shattered. I lay awake most of the night, deeply moved and overwhelmed by previously unshed tears of grief and sorrow.

A few days later Tom and I met an extraordinary family who had one biological son and one adopted son from India. We went home from that chance meeting feeling inspired and curiously fascinated by the whole notion of being able to love and care for an adopted child.

Five months after that meeting, Tom and I attended an orientation meeting at a well-known agency that specializes in international adoption. After listening to the stories of some of the "waiting children," we knew what we wanted to do. We left the meeting, much later, clutching a precious Polaroid of a four-and-a-half-year-old boy from Khabaravosk, Russia. The boy's name was Anatoly, and his smile was contagious. All we knew about him was that he had been in orphanages since birth. Our decision to make this child our son would be made with full acceptance of the risks of the unknown. My Eastern European roots certainly penetrated into Russia, and I felt the miraculous hope of new life where there had always been a barren wasteland of sad emptiness. We signed the necessary paperwork, and our family began to prepare

these nameless and faceless children in search of a family to which they could belong.

As an adult my life was full and rich, and these images began to fade. Then I, along with millions of

psychologically for the arrival of our new family member, a son.

It was Tom who was elected to travel to Russia to bring Tolya home. He later wrote in his journal:

I began my journey to Russia six months after we fell in love with the picture of Anatoly. With each day my resolve to bring him home became stronger. My small group of adoptive parents and I were detained in Moscow, waiting for airline tickets to Siberia. It was a dark, cold, snowy night when we, along with a planeful of passengers and animals, boarded an Aeroflot jet for our destination. It was to have been a nine-hour flight with no food service or any of the amenities we were accustomed to. Shortly after boarding we began to smell smoke. For the next three hours we watched men carry parts on and off the plane. I don't know how I got the courage to stay on that shaky-looking airplane. I guess I knew that it would be the only way to get my son. At this point we code-named the trip "child quest."

Approximately fifteen hours after boarding, we landed in Khabaravosk. Finally, I was only an hour away from seeing my son. My only real hope was that he would love me as much as I knew I loved him. I hoped that his having been institutionalized for his whole life had not shut down his ability to love. I was excited . . . scared. When our van ran out of gas we were stuck on the side of the road for hours. It became too late to go to the orphanage that day, and we checked into a hotel, of sorts.

After a long, sleepless night we finally arrived at the orphanage. I was flying. We met the director and were escorted to meet our children. I walked into a large, beautifully decorated room occupied by twelve happy and beautiful children.

Alexandra Nikolai called out Tolya's name, and a little boy turned around and looked at me with bright eyes and an inquisitive smile. He walked over to me with all of his friends. I knelt down and said, "Tolya, ya tavoy papa." We embraced and he kissed me on the cheek. I was overwhelmed with feeling. I was completely and unconditionally in love with this little person. All went well, and as I was about to take this loving, adorable, and happy boy with me, his caretaker asked him if he was ready to leave the orphanage with me. Tolya looked back and forth at us, took hold of my hand, and replied in Russian, "I shall go with my papa." I guess this is as close as any man can come to the experience a woman has giving birth. I was on top of the world.

Six days later we landed back in Albuquerque. Lots of friends and family were at the airport to greet us. Joanne, Ariel, and Alexi were ecstatic. They loved him as much as I did. But most touching of all was to watch Joanne's parents greeting Tolya in Russian—a language they hadn't spoken since the Holocaust.

Seeing Tolya for the first time and embracing his sweet, little, courageous self filled me with such love! I was completely ready to begin the adventure of weaving his life with ours, in the mysterious way families are formed. That first night, after feeding and bathing him, we put him in his bed and kissed him goodnight. His look of openness and vulnerability was unforgettable. As I was leaving his room he cried out, "Mama!" When I turned around, he was on his knees with outstretched arms.

The months following Tolya's arrival were both a joy and a challenge. It took a while for all of us to strike a new balance, and we all worked hard to show him what it is like to live in a family. Some of our best times took place during visits to my parents' house. The first time Tolya called my dad *Dadushka* ("grandfather") he cried. He had not heard that name—the name he had used for his own grandfather—for fifty years. As for my mom, she began dreaming about Russian people who had occupied her village in Poland before the Nazis invaded, and the permission she accorded herself to dream brought its own kind of healing.

It is perhaps no coincidence that the orphaned, like those who lost everything and those who went out into the world in search of asylum after World War II, are often called survivors. The richness of Tolya's heritage has enriched our own, bringing with it a sense of completion and peace to our family—an unexpected blessing.

A born survivor, Tolya has been part of our family for five years now. In three years we plan to take him back to Russia for his Bar Mitzvah. There, in the oldest synagogue in Moscow—one filled with haunting memories of generations who have gone before him—Tolya will stand as a man in the country of his birth, surrounded by those who love him.

POSTSCRIPT: Since adopting Tolya, Joanne and Tom have had a strong urge to "spread the word." In 1997 they made a documentary portraying life in the Russian orphanage system. The film made its debut at the prestigious Sundance Film Festival in January 1998, where it was highly acclaimed, and was featured in The Second Annual International Family Film Festival in Albuquerque in May, 1998.

Three Generations

IRENE, RONNIE, AND BRIANNA KASSORLA
HOLMBY HILLS, CALIFORNIA

In 1990, when Ronnie—with the love, help, and support of her mother, Irene—decided to become a single mother, they were blessed with a remarkably easy adoption. Less than forty-eight hours after first meeting with an adoption attorney, Brianna Irene was placed in their arms. Irene has taken an active role in raising her namesake, from dropping Brianna at school daily to hosting weekly sleepovers at her home. Ronnie and Irene are now ready to become a mother and grandmother again, but after three long years of searching, they have not found another baby to adopt.

RONNIE: It still absolutely amazes me when I think about how quickly Brianna came into our lives. As I hit my mid thirties, divorced and not in a relationship, I started to seriously think about becoming a single mother. I had tried to get pregnant during a long-term relationship, but unfortunately it didn't happen, and the man and I eventually broke up. My inability to conceive at that time may have been caused by scarring from an IUD that had been inserted many years ago and ultimately had to have surgically removed. So in October 1990 my mother and I decided to explore the possibility of adoption. The two of us are extremely close, and I was living in her guest house at the time. I remember the phone call I made to her that night. She had just finished an appearance on the five o'clock news talking about family relationships, and I asked her for her help and support.

IRENE: That next Friday we went to see an adoption attorney for what we thought would be an exploratory meeting. I assumed that it would take a year or longer to actually get a baby. At first the attorney was not at all supportive and was very reluctant to even consider trying to find a baby for a single mother, as so many birth mothers want their child to be placed with a two-parent family. It was as if he considered us a waste of time. But as we continued to talk something magical happened, and we all connected on some sort of stronger level. Ronnie was no longer just one more hopeful parent but a woman who deeply wanted to be a mother and was deeply committed to becoming one. Two hours later we were all in tears as Ronnie and I bared our souls to this man who had been a total stranger.

He then told us that he knew a birth mother who was nine months pregnant and had just started slow labor. She had not yet been matched with adoptive parents, as she had been planning to keep her baby until only very recently. The birth mother had taken the bus to Los Angeles that morning from her home, three hours away. Our attorney felt that since a single mother had raised her, she might be open to placing her baby with a single mother. Ronnie and I were flabbergasted and excited at the same time. This was not at all how we had envisioned getting a baby, but we decided to meet the birth mother then and there. That night we quickly arranged for a family powwow to decide if we should go forward. Everyone agreed to bring this soon-to-be-born child into our family!

RONNIE: We got called at 3 A.M. from the birth mother, telling us that she was going into hard labor. After getting dressed in less than five minutes, my mother, sister Jackie, and I picked her up at her hotel and took her to the hospital. The three of us spent the next eleven hours with her. During that time I really began to respect the birth mother. She had everything that I admire in a person—a good mind, a sense of humor, an incredibly sweetness—but she had never had the kind of opportunities that I have had. Mother and I were in the labor room to help with the first big push. Several pushes later, an absolutely beautiful and angelic head appeared.

I stayed with her and my new daughter, Brianna Irene, all night long and Saturday morning. My mother was hosting a huge party for a political candidate she was endorsing that night and couldn't help me get ready to bring Brianna home. I didn't even have a crib and couldn't take Brianna out of the hospital until I found an infant car seat. It all happened so quickly; I was not prepared. I purchased a pink stroller, and she slept in that for the first month until I could get organized!

IRENE: There is something so rewarding about helping to raise a baby at my age. I am so much

because she is our daughter and granddaughter. In turn, Brianna seems to respect other people and us. She is a good citizen and almost never breaks a rule. We are an extremely close family, and I love being with my girls.

RONNIE: Mother probably spends more quality time with Brianna than I do. She is such a great grandmother. Our family is filled with so much happiness and laughter since Brianna has arrived. I can't remember ever having laughed so much. It's those little moments that are not meaningful to anyone else that are so important to us. I believe that Brianna came into our lives by divine intervention. In a sense I believe that I was "chosen" to be her mother.

Unfortunately, as easy and painless as it was to bring Brianna into our family, it has been incredibly frustrating and difficult to find another child. We have been hoping to adopt again for more than two years and have run into so many problems and stumbling blocks. Our obvious choice was Brianna's birth mother, but because of the complications of that birth she did not want to carry another child for us. One birth mother decided to keep her baby six months into her pregnancy, and many others told me that they had taken drugs during their pregnancies. But we haven't given up hope and would still love to have a brother or sister for Brianna.

wiser now and have more time to spend with Brianna. Success came to me at a very young age, but the joy that my little granddaughter has given to me is almost indescribable. I take her to school every morning and plan my appointments, and sometimes my life, around her. Ronnie and I love being with her because she's such a delight. There is nowhere else in my life that I would rather be than with Brianna. She also spends Saturdays with me; we go to plays, museums, or movies. At night my husband and I always plan a special dinner and evening out.

I think we have a real appreciation of her—we respect and value Brianna as a person and not just

IRENE: Forty years ago it was such a financial struggle. Although I opted to stay home with my children for the first few years, after my first husband and I divorced I went back to night school and studied to become a doctor with a degree in psychology. My life is so much different now than it was when I was raising my own two daughters. I have literally helped to raise more than a thousand children through my work, but I wanted someone that I could truly love—a child of my own. Helping to raise Brianna is such a joy. She is such a miracle and truly the center of my heart and world. God truly gave us a gift.

Will the "Real" Dad Please Stand Up?

GLENN AND DONNA MILLER
NEWTON, NEW JERSEY

To what lengths does a stepfather have to go to be considered a "real" father? For eight years Glenn Miller raised his wife's three children, providing the financial and emotional support one might expect of any responsible parent. He was their father in fact if not their father by law. His commitment was real, full-time, and permanent. But legal? Well . . .

I WAS STILL IN HIGH SCHOOL when I married my first husband. Five years and three children later I was raising my kids alone and working two jobs to keep a roof over their heads. It was a difficult but not altogether unfamiliar role. I, too, had been born to a young mother who, although ill-prepared to raise her family alone, took on the task and did her best. Then I met Glenn Miller, single, hard-working, raised by his working mother after his parents divorced when he was just seven. From the start he admired my spunk and determination to keep my family together. It was something he understood—and respected. We dated. We lived together. Eventually we married. And when seven-year-old Trisha, the oldest of my three children, asked him if they could all call him "Dad," he agreed. That was, after all, really how it was.

Glenn knew that kids need love, patience, and fun in their lives if they are going to grow up to be responsible and have their heads on right. He loved being outdoors and could usually be found puttering at odd jobs around our home. This was a natural come-on to the kids, and Glenn usually had a crew of eager, if not quite accomplished, helpers trailing after him.

By the time all three had entered school, they were Millers in their *minds,* if not legally on the registration forms in the office. It was Glenn, after all, who was their mainstay. He was the dad who cheered for them on the playing field, checked their homework each evening, and spent time with them. For eight years Glenn was truly their father in fact, if not their father by law. That all changed, however, when Trisha turned sixteen and wanted to apply for her driver's permit. "I don't want to put Trisha Ford on my application, Dad," she said. "I want to be Trisha Miller *for real.*" What was a father to do?

The next day I called a local lawyer to see what would be required to allow Glenn to legally adopt the three children who already called him "Dad." "Why bother?" he asked. "The kids are almost grown." Needless to say, he didn't get my business. After several other calls we learned that it can be costly to do the right thing for a child—even at the child's request. Glenn would need to be interviewed and studied by a caseworker from a licensed adoption agency, and a report evaluating his capacity to parent Trisha, James, and Jamie would have to be filed with the court, approved, and accepted. This made me more determined than ever, and I called several adoption agencies and explained our situation. Apparently touched by our story, one agreed to see us right away and even reduced their customary fees so the process could go forward immediately.

Finally it happened. The Miller family—all five of us, standing together—had our day in court. By agreeing to let Glenn adopt the three children he had already raised for eight years, the State of New Jersey would certify that my husband, Glenn Allen Miller, forty-six, was their *real and permanent father,* both emotionally and legally. Other than the inconvenience, frustration, stacks of paperwork, and expense involved, the decree was merely a technicality. The kids already knew who their real father was. Two weeks later, Trish *Miller* got her driver's license.

First . . . A Little Sweetheart from Bangladesh

DAVID AND DONNA CLAUSS
BELEN, NEW MEXICO

O NE OF THE WONDERFUL THINGS about prospective adoptive parents is their innocence and blind faith as they approach the process of becoming a family. My husband, David, and I were no exception. In 1976 we were living in England and teaching at the Department of Defense schools there. Eager to start a family and naive about the adoption process, we thought all we needed to do to get a child was to select an interesting foreign country and apply. Wrong!

Simple eligibility requirements helped us narrow down our choices. Shortly after the war-torn region of Bangladesh emerged as a new country, we supported fund-raising efforts for social welfare projects there. We felt connected to and

International adoption affords parents a unique worldview. Donna and David Clauss have six children, from Bangladesh, Mexico, Vietnam, and Korea. Their experience and commitment to children led them to start Rainbow House International, an adoption agency organized to find loving families for orphaned and abandoned children around the world. Although this is Rokeya's story, it also conveys the longings of other parents who are willing to search the world over for a child to love and raise.

compassion for the Bangladeshi people, so with blind faith and not a moment of hesitation we poured all of our passion and adoption energy into Bangladesh. Bangladesh was well represented by their embassy staff in London. I immediately found help from a consular officer who assisted us in obtaining all the required forms to adopt a child through the government-administered Inter-Country Adoption Project. We were on our way at last.

Completing the application was as overwhelming then as it is for adoptive parents today, but obtaining a home study from a licensed agency and a letter of government approval proved to be even more challenging. As U.S. citizens living and working abroad, it was all but impossible to find an agency that would complete the necessary home study. Desperately exploring alternatives, I found a base chaplain who had adopted from Vietnam, and although he was not a social worker, he at least had some personal experience with international adoption. I put him in touch with a worker at the U.S. base where we taught and scoured the libraries of Oxford University until I found an appropriate home-study outline. Together the valiant team prepared the magic document to the satisfaction of the Bangladesh government.

Over and over again we encountered obstacles that looked like mountains but were eventually reduced to a pebble on the parenthood path. On the one hand, the British politely declined our request for a relevant letter of government approval. On the other hand, the New Mexico Department of Human Services did so with ease and grace. We had to redo our application when the first one was apparently lost. Whereas these detours were frustrating and time-consuming, nothing could have prepared us for the next exasperating part of our adoption. As we prepared to return to the States for the summer, I approached the British Home Office to initiate entry clearance procedures so our Bangladeshi child could be issued a visa that would allow her to enter Great Britain and join us. For the first time in my life I experienced real prejudice when I didn't even get a response. We left England with no referral and no assurance that we would even be allowed to bring our child into England.

Back in the States, the summer dragged on. Then, in August, we received an excited call from our neighbor in England. In between sobs, Pat read the long-awaited letter: "Mr. And Mrs. Clauss, we are sorry that it has taken some time to find an appropriate child, but we are happy to inform you that we now have a beautiful baby daughter, Rokeya, for you. We hope to be able to send her in two months." There were no other details.

Two months passed with no news of our daughter. Thanksgiving came and went and Christmas loomed. I passed my days in shopping

malls, looking for infants the same age as our Rokeya so I could experience vicariously this age and stage of her development. Valentine's Day came and went. The closet was overflowing with clothes purchased, knitted, and made for each passing season; furniture was hand made and painted and a room prepared in the cheeriest of colors. I was sure

they would never be used, though, as our daughter was growing older with each passing week. Each night ended with a thousand kisses blown to the East and many tears shed as I wondered who was holding her tonight and singing her lullabies.

Then, with Easter approaching, the phone rang with the news that our daughter was scheduled to arrive in Canada on March 18 and continue on to Chicago the next day. Never was an airline ticket acquired faster. I arrived at the airline gate three hours early and paced back and forth, in the final stages of "labor," exactly nine months after her day of birth.

The flight arrived and the passengers deplaned—but no babies. In tears, I boarded the plane to look for the missing passengers along with another anxious mother who was waiting to greet her son. From the plane's bulkhead came a cacophony of baby cries from nineteen teeny, tiny bodies identified only by the names on their hospital wristbands. As I looked around frantically, a gentle, middle-aged man stepped forward with a gorgeous baby. He had boarded the plane in Montreal and, drawn to this little girl with her loveliest of personalities, hadn't been able to put her down the entire trip. With fear and a silent hope I searched her wristband. Yes, oh yes, it was her! She was more beautiful, more gentle, more endearing than any dream or imagination could conjure. With many thank-yous to the countless volunteers who had brought her around the world, we were on our way to meet Daddy.

The first challenge to our commitment and our dreams of parenthood came less than twenty-four hours after Rokeya arrived in our arms. Weighing barely seven pounds, our daughter was grievously ill. Our pediatrician debated whether or not to put her immediately in the hospital but wisely feared that one more abrupt institutionalization might cause her to give up her will to live. In response, we rallied to the occasion. Every second was used to provide this baby with hope, a will to live, and a belief that today could be fun and tomorrow even more promising. The miracle of antibiotics, the power of love, a great doctor, and soulful lullabies all contributed to helping our little one bounce back quickly. And all of the clothes we had accumulated fit.

Our commitment to becoming a family of three expanded to becoming a family of eight over the years. I chuckle each time someone remarks that adoption is the "easy road" to becoming parents. The timid and meek should not proceed. Many times over the last twenty years our commitment had been challenged. Our Rokeya is now in her junior year at the university, on a full presidential scholarship. One day she hopes to be an occupational therapist specializing in sensory-integration problems in children. Our work has come full circle, and I would gladly take the challenge all over again. Without this child we would have laughed only half of our laughs, shed only half of our tears, and seen only a partial view of this world.

Namaste! Greetings!

SENATOR JOHN AND MRS. CINDY McCAIN
PHOENIX, ARIZONA

Into most lives will walk an unexpected opportunity—a "yea" or "nay" moment that can change things forever. For Senator John McCain (R-AZ) and his wife, Cindy, that opportunity came in the body of a tiny ten-week-old infant from Bangladesh who needed immediate medical care to survive. Here is how they answered that call and a description of the impact that adoption decision had on their lives.

IN ALL HONESTY, adoption was never part of our plan, although children certainly were. We had three delightful ones—Meghan, Jack, and Jimmy. With John traveling most weekends between Phoenix and Washington so he could be home with his family, we learned early on how to manage our time wisely. The happiness and satisfaction of each family member was, after all, important to the happiness of the whole.

I, too, was busy, not only with the demands of family and public life but also with fund-raising for a nonprofit organization I started in 1987. The goal was to send volunteer medical teams from our country to help children right in the countries where they were living. In some cases, when a child's medical condition required more intervention than could be supported in a single surgery, we arranged for the child's care back in the States, with volunteer families providing nurturing interim care and support until the child could return home.

In 1992 I accompanied a medical team for ten weeks as they worked night and day at an orphanage run by Mother Teresa in Bangladesh. Stretched to the limit, understaffed, overworked, and with new arrivals abandoned and left in baskets outside the door of the infirmary every day, the Sisters calmly went about the job of caring for 160 newborns. Most of these tiny babies weighed less than three pounds and came into the world already showing the ravages of poor nutrition and disease passed on to them before birth. Many were born with congenital anomalies—clubbed feet and hands, heart defects, cleft palates—that would make them outcasts beyond the orphanage gates even if they did survive. It was both a heart-wrenching and an inspirational experience. If love alone could have saved each and every tiny body, these babies certainly would have been infused with life.

As we worked around the clock to treat and stabilize as many of the babies as we could, I found myself drawn to one tiny little girl whose huge brown eyes filled her face as they followed me. Below those eyes was a gaping hole in her lip and palate. "Couldn't we repair it?" I asked. But hers was a complicated cleft that would require several surgeries. We needed to obtain a medical visa for her immediately while I made arrangements for her surgical procedures and long-term care with a family back in the United States. All services and care

would be volunteered, with no compensation other than her beautiful smile at completion.

Babies have a funny way of upending the best-laid plans of organized adults. As our group of medically fragile infants and escorts prepared to leave for home, I could think only of the brown-eyed beauty cradled in my arms, not her uncertain future. I'll get there first and worry about the future later, I thought as I boarded the plane. She needs these surgeries! Rarely sleeping during the long and exhausting trip, she stared up confidently at me with those big brown eyes. She already knew what I did not. She was on her way home to an unsuspecting dad, two brothers, and a sister—and she was cuddled up in her mom's arms at that very moment. Over the coming years when she would ask how she came to our family, I would say, "The angels gave you to us, Bridget." And surely, surely, I knew on that day that they did.

Once officially in the McCain starting gate, Bridget, as we named her, was ready for the race. She was a trooper throughout the extensive medical procedures necessary to close and repair her lip and palate, and she tolerated (most of the time!) hours of speech therapy. When she entered kindergarten last fall and some children made an issue of her speech and dark skin color, her siblings could not understand the teasing. But they realized that despite their having embraced her, Bridget was not invisible to the world that lay outside the protection and security of our family. My own training was in the field of special education, yet I, too, was caught off guard as I worked with her to help her catch up to her peers without jeopardizing her self-esteem and self-confidence. It provided a lesson and a larger view for all of us.

In most ways, however, we are a typical American family. We like to be together, to read together, to play together, and to tell stories to one another. Now that the children are a little older, John is beginning to share some of his own painful stories and memories of his experience as a prisoner of war in Vietnam after being shot down over Hanoi in 1967. It's easy to take our lives for granted. It takes work to be a healthy and vibrant family. Families can drift apart if they become lulled into complacency and stop communicating with one another. Active, closely bonded, and loving, each person here works to achieve a delicate balance between work and play, public life and private life, family time and one-to-one time. We are all committed to that effort. So far, we have all benefited.

NOTE: Now serving in the 105th Congress, Senator McCain is chairman of the Senate Commerce, Science, and Transportation Committee and serves on the Armed Services and Indian Affairs Committees. He has been chairman of the International Republican Institute (IRI) since 1993.

Emma Has Two Mothers

CONNIE BRACKTENBACH AND VICKY McGREGOR
MANITOU SPRINGS, COLORADO

When Connie and Vicky got together seven years ago they both decided that they wanted a child. Vicky had never had a desire to get pregnant so it was Connie who decided to be inseminated by donor sperm. Getting pregnant was easy, but she lost the baby in her seventh month. Both women were devastated but decided to try again immediately before grief and depression drove them apart. A wonderful man volunteered to be the donor, and Emma Bracktenbach was born nine months later.

CONNIE: One of my earliest childhood memories, from when I was about three, is of standing in the bathroom, looking into a mirror, and telling my parents that I wanted a baby when I grew up. They of course responded that I had to get much older and be married first. But even as a little girl I was never interested in boys or getting married and felt that if I thought about a baby long and hard it would happen. And it did sort of happen that way. When Vicky and I got together seven years ago I knew that I eventually wanted to have a child with her. As I was only twenty-five, we were in no hurry to get pregnant, but I had sort of set thirty as my biological deadline. Three years later we felt that we were ready for this kind of commitment, and my life-long desire was about to be realized—I would carry the child.

VICKY: I was married for five years before meeting Connie and had mixed feel-

gle brother to see if he would be interested in donor sperm insemination. But we all agreed that it could get kind of weird, with my parents not knowing they had a biological grandchild—and how would we tell our child who its father was? So we ultimately decided to go to a sperm bank. We were so naive that we contacted an organization and said we simply wanted to buy some sperm. Wrong. Sperm is only administered by a certified health care professional. It became kind of fun to pick out the biological father. He was a young Brazilian donor, and we dreamed about a dark-skinned, exotic, green-eyed beauty.

CONNIE: The insemination itself was incredibly easy, but I lost the baby in the seventh month. Vicky and I were devastated and couldn't believe such a problem-free pregnancy could end this way. This child had been our hope and fantasy for three years. Knowing she would be a girl, we had already named her Rosalie. Two weeks before miscarrying I had a premonition, this amazing dream in which Rosalie was running through our house, turned toward me, and became a butterfly. We were still in mourning when a remarkable man stepped into our lives. He had heard our story and volunteered to be a donor when we were ready to try again. The father of four daughters, all he wanted to know was when the baby had been born and if it was healthy. We were incredibly moved but didn't know if we

ings about children. But one thing was certain—I never wanted to get pregnant. Several years into our relationship Connie and I started to seriously talk about having a child; even though we were in a nontraditional relationship, we didn't want to be out of the family loop. Initially we approached my sin-

could face another pregnancy so soon after such heartbreak.

VICKY: Connie had gone back to work but was in a terrible depression. I tried to be as strong as I could, but I began to feel disconnected from her. We both felt that if we waited a year or two to get pregnant again we might not do it. So we turned right around and decided to bring our dream of a child to life. Connie, whom I nicknamed Fertile Myrtle, got pregnant again on the first insemination. We both had a very different feeling this time. I was trying to be as supportive as I could be, but losing Rosalie had made me realize that babies do die.

CONNIE: And I was scared and worried the whole time. This wasn't the carefree pregnancy I had experienced with Rosalie. It seemed to last forever. The insemination was done at home and was as easy as it had been the first time. Presto, a month later I was pregnant. I don't think that you ever get over the loss of a child, even if it hasn't been born yet. We still, on occasion, hit an emotional wall. But I had a relatively easy birth, and our daughter, beautiful Emma Bracktenbach, was born at home on September 26, 1994. The birth was surrounded by a soft-white light, and Emma has been the light of our lives ever since. Emma has beautiful green eyes, just like we had imagined, and has taught us both so much over the last three years. She has adjusted completely to having two mothers and calls me "Mommy" and Vicky "Mamma."

VICKY: We live in this wonderful Victorian house in the Colorado mountains. Connie, Emma, and I live on the first floor, and our best friends, another female couple, live upstairs. Neither Connie nor I have a close relationship with our parents; this is our family. We have made a lifelong commitment to each other and truly became a family when Emma was born. Even though Emma and I do not have a biological connection, I couldn't love her any more and hope to see my grandchildren through her. We have a single mother and daughter who live next door and several other children on our block who all support and look out for one another.

My one fear is that there will be some parents at Emma's school who won't let their children play with her because we are lesbians. And that's sad, because they will never know us and how much we truly love Emma.

Part IV

Pioneers Share

Their Wisdom

....

T HERE IS MUCH wisdom to be gained from the six pioneers whose stories make up this final chapter of *Parents at Last*. Their experiences give us glimpses of what is possible on the path to parenthood and the outcome of some of those experiences. We can use their examples as guides. All of the adoptive parents speak warmly of the gift their children gave them—the opportunity to share their lives, love, and resources—and of the changing attitudes toward adoption in the last half of this century. Their children are now grown. Some are young adults just starting out; others are "baby boomers" rapidly approaching middle age. The simple acts of blind faith by their pioneering parents helped to set their own course.

The two adult adoptees, whose first-hand experience with adoption spans nearly seventy years, are the "children" that allowed two couples to be called "mom" and "dad." Their reflections help us understand how they feel about those choices and how adoption has impacted their lives. Clearly, they value their adoptive families in all their strengths and their imperfections; no family is ever perfect. Adoptive parents will feel reassured of their importance in the lives of their children, but they are asked to be sensitive to the often unspoken concerns and anxieties of their adopted children. Many adoptees long to look into the face of another human being who resembles them. Adoptees may have to wait to find that longing satisfied until they can gaze into the face of their *own* children and grandchildren, if not ever directly into the face of their own birthmother. Looking expectantly to the future rather than longingly at the past is a valuable insight for adoptive parents to be able to offer to their own adopted child at times of such longing.

Finally, the story of one single mother whose decision to conceive and raise a child in the seventies when this was a radical departure from generally accepted practice proves that the biological drive can be stronger than the threat of public disapproval. Her story reminds us that we must trust our intuitions, seek the best information available, and not always cave in to the opinions of others when we are deciding what is best for us. Creative solutions to the problems of infertility are not new, but public acceptance of the choices available to those seeking parenthood today shows greater understanding and compassion.

Looking Back on Twenty-Five Years of Adoptive Parenting

MEL AND BETSY HAAS

FAIR HAVEN, NEW JERSEY

Mel and Betsy Haas made a conscious decision to put their family first and their careers second as they went about building their family of six—three boys and three girls from Korea—in the 1970s. Today their justifiable pride in the caring young adult that each has become is a clear testament to that decision.

ADOPTION HAS DEFINED the greater part of our adult lives. When we began that journey almost thirty years ago we could not have known how grateful we'd be one day for the opportunity to parent six such terrific young people. Looking back at what we learned as parents through all the growing stages of our life as a family, certain things stand out.

We quickly learned that flexibility was fundamental to family success, no matter how a family is formed. As our kids grew, we had to learn to go with the flow—or drown. It's impossible to force children (no matter how they become your children) into blindly following what you want them to do or be. Since every child is different, we tried to make time to recognize and respect each one. We learned that what works for one child won't necessarily work for another. Our family created a mighty big gene pool when we gathered around the dining room table, so we worked hard to value difference and diversity yet remain true to the values and standards we believed were important. We tried to establish rules that we felt were necessary to create a home that respected the rights of each member and avoided power struggles over little things. The problems and challenges we faced along the way were rarely the ones for which we had prepared. We lived with messy rooms, odd hair styles and colors, bizarre eating habits, and talents and abilities that were new to us. We were challenged, we did worry, we did learn, and we did grow.

We learned to be proactive on behalf of each child. We had to be their strong advocates in many arenas—school, medical care, and community. Who else is better able to lovingly monitor a child's well-being than a concerned parent? As parents of six children from Korea, we often had to push for special services such as English as a Second Language or other temporary support services. I frequently found myself in the awkward position of having to educate—sensitize—both teachers and the school administration to adoption issues that affected our children in school. It seemed easier for school officials to put the kids into the slots the school was used to—a class for the learning disabled, for example—when what was needed was help with language skills. I will never forget (or forgive) the teacher who said to me after our six-year-old had been here about five months, "But Mrs. Haas, he doesn't know his vowels!" I smiled, through gritted teeth, and replied, "But Mrs. ____, he doesn't even know his English."

Sometimes seemingly innocuous things, such as the wording on standard forms, lack sensitivity to the child who joins his family through adoption. One form at our school requires parents to define their status in relation to the child. The choices are "natural," "step," "foster," and "other." We refused to be an "other" so always checked "natural" and just let the school figure it out. It seemed to be the closest to the kind of relationship we have, even though our kids are Asian.

When we first adopted it was still unusual for families in the United States to adopt from overseas. We found that medical matters involving our children often required special attention and advocacy. Most doctors did not know how to evaluate the health issues and needs of an internationally adopted child and randomly applied U.S. standards and expectations in completing their assessments. The result was often inadequate plans for treating our children. We learned how important it could be to seek out second opinions and to trust our parental intuition. Fortunately for today's adoptive families there is a wealth of expert information available to provide local physicians and adoptive families direction.

We found that we needed to be sensitive to the subtle racism and discrimination that existed in our community and to seize all opportunities to educate others. Sometimes this meant changing schools, communities, social groups, or places of worship. Sometimes it meant taking ethnic food into church potluck dinners or offering to talk to groups about adoption. It also meant being willing to stand up at work and speak out when a remark was made about adoption or our children's race or ethnic background. We made sure the library had positive books about adoption for children and adults. We also joined local adoptive-family support groups, even though we didn't consider ourselves "joiners."

Finally, we consciously chose to put our family first, even though it meant slowing down our careers for a time. After all, wanting a family is what brought us to adoption in the first place. We knew that we would only have our children for a few short years, so it was important to do what was right for them. We moved to a community with a good school system rather than to the house with the prettiest view. We missed parties at work to attend "Back to School Night." We declined to help out someone in the extended family in order to be at a game that was important to our sports-crazy kids. We made ourselves available to chauffeur our kids and their friends, and we made sure our house was never empty on a Saturday night. We found we needed to be around and present. We needed to be involved, in both unobtrusive and visible ways.

We learned most of this as we went along. It might have been helpful had we known a few more things when we began our adoption journey. It would have been nice to know with greater certainty that I didn't need to be perfect and that it wasn't possible to be all things to all people. I wish I had worried less about whether the children would survive if I had a messy house, served canned soup for dinner, or made mistakes in doling out consequences for misbehavior. It also might have been comforting to know that there is no such thing as a perfect family and that I didn't have to "fix" everything for everyone. Nonetheless, we did our best and loved the children with all our hearts. When we did what we thought was right and loved and respected them totally, things usually worked out reasonably well.

Ironically, I think the main thing that I wish I had known was how thankful we would be that our path to parenthood led us to the decision to adopt. Watching each of these children grow into wonderful adults has been the most important part of our lives.

Sisterly Love

CONGRESSWOMAN CONNIE MORELLA
WASHINGTON, D.C.

In an act of deep love and commitment, Congresswoman Connie Morella and her husband, Tony, adopted six nieces and nephews after the death of her sister, Mary, from cancer in 1975. Mary's children joined the Morellas' three biological children to create a warm and loving extended family. Though all nine children have since left home, Congresswoman Morella remains a strong children's advocate in Congress.

I REMEMBER THE DAY VIVIDLY, even though it was almost twenty-five years ago. My little sister, Mary, hadn't been feeling well for months and finally decided to be admitted to a Boston hospital for some tests. We were holding hands and talking when the doctor came into the hospital room and grimly told Mary that she had terminal cancer that had spread to her lymph nodes. He guessed that she had six months, perhaps a year, to live. All the color drained from my face, and I felt like I was in the theater of the absurd, with no way out. I hugged Mary close and we both cried.

At thirty-eight, Mary was just starting to get her life back together again. Recently divorced, she had six children under sixteen and was extremely proud that she had successfully reentered the workplace. Mary's ex-husband could not face her prognosis, so I was the one who told their children about their mother's illness and what would happen to her as she underwent chemotherapy. My sister

lost all her beautiful hair and was in and out of the hospital. I moved into her home, hired a nurse, and stayed with her and the children until she died at home almost two years later, in July 1976.

There was never any question that we wouldn't take the children and raise them as our own. My husband, Tony, is an attorney, and we got guardianship of all six boys and girls. Her ex-husband didn't want to or could not handle the responsibility of being a single father.

In August we all moved back to Maryland to join Tony and our three biological children and started to redesign our rather modest home. We now had nine children between the ages of ten and twenty. The family room and two studies were turned into four very small bedrooms.

At that time Paul, our oldest, was in college, Mark was a young teenager, and Laura was about twelve. Mary's oldest, Christine, was ready to start her senior year in high school; the twins, Louise and Catherine, were sixteen, Paul was fifteen, Rachel was thirteen, and Ursula was just ten. In the beginning home life was extremely chaotic, and I had to depend on friends with children the same age as ours to help with child care.

Paul, Mark, and Laura were just fabulous. They had to give up a lot of the attention they had been accustomed to receiving when there were just five of us. They seemed to realize that this was the right thing to do. I had to organize the chores quickly. We

bought a new washer and dryer, got each child a laundry hamper, and except for the youngest, had them do their own laundry. We closed our eyes to the dust in the corners and the dirty dishes that were constantly in the sink.

During these early years I was teaching at Montgomery College and had started to become involved in politics. Once, when running for an appointed position in the state legislature, I was asked by one of the men who was evaluating the candidates, "Do you think that you can handle all the responsibilities of the legislature and your extended family?" I knew right then that I would not get the appointment, even though I had all the credentials for the position. I was right. If I had been a man I'm sure I would have been lauded for my family commitment, and my wife would probably have been home with the kids. Twenty-five years ago there weren't that many women in politics. When my son Mark put a bumper sticker on his locker that said "People for Morella," a buddy asked him what office his father was running for. He was furious, as our family believed and practiced total equality: dishes, laundry, yardwork, and car washing were done by everyone. With a family of eleven there was no room for prima donnas.

I have to give Tony a lot of credit for making our family work. Family has always been very important to him, and he completely supported my desire to adopt Mary's children. Their biological father did not have much involvement with his children after they came to live with us. It's amazing to me that he denied himself the benefit of these wonderful kids who have so greatly enriched our lives. He sends them an occasional letter and birthday card but has remarried and now lives in California. They call us "Mom" and "Dad," and we truly consider them our own. When the girls got married Tony walked them all down the aisle. We even managed to send all nine children to college, with the help of loans, financial aid, and their own hard work.

The kids thought that I was the tougher parent and nicknamed me "The Scrutinizer," as I was always asking questions about their friends and romances. I also demanded that we all stick to schedules so that we could get places in our old rattletrap of a station wagon almost on time. It was me who took all nine of them to take their driver's tests and get their licenses.

Because family has always been so important to Tony and me, I have become something of a children's advocate in Congress. I am the cosponsor of legislation to help families who make too much money to be eligible for Medicare but don't make enough money to afford decent health care. I am also very involved with legislation to stop domestic violence. Each year almost four million children see one parent abuse the other, and spousal abuse is a direct result of earlier child abuse. We must put a value on people so that they will value themselves.

Today we have fifteen grandchildren, and the kids still stick together and help one another. Even though our family is now scattered across the country, we are still incredibly close. We talk on the phone almost every day and are very involved with, but never interfere in, one another's lives. For us, our family has created a life-long unity and strength. My sister, who died so young, taught me how precious each day is and how you have to live it to the fullest. I frequently think about the moment in the movie *Zorba the Greek* when a friend tells Zorba that he lives like he is going to live forever and Zorba responds, "I live like I might die at any minute."

Mary left us way too soon, and we will always miss her. But she left behind such a wonderful legacy—her children!

A Chosen Life

HOLLEE MCGINNIS

NEW YORK CITY

When a family chooses an international adoption, they change future generations of their family forever. Hollee McGinnis, Korean in appearance but definitely Irish-German-American in her soul, found her own direction by bridging both worlds and creating "a.k.a.," a promising new support organization for transcultural, transracial adoptees like herself. This helped her define a strong new identity that honors both her birth and her adoption.

AT THE HEART OF ADOPTION IS CHOICE. To *adopt* is defined as "to take by choice into a relationship" and implies "accepting something created by another or foreign to one's nature." I was adopted at age three from Korea, and as a young adult I came to reflect on how my life had been shaped by the decisions of others—my birth mother's decision to bear me; my birth father's decision to put me up for adoption; my adoptive parents' decision to expand their love across oceans, nations, and races—and the fact that I did not have a say in any of those choices. However, I did have a choice of my own to make. I had a choice in what my adoption would mean to me. It was during my own search for meaning that I started an organization that seeks to recognize the community of people whose lives, through adoption, have bridged nations, cultures, and races and to embrace the possibility of a future that celebrates our common humanity and diversity.

Although I always knew I had been born in Korea and adopted, I was not always conscious of what either of these meant. As I was growing up, being Korean described my physical appearance, explained where I came from, and made me unique within my family. As a teenager I became more conscious of looking Asian. I realized that because of my physical appearance people assumed I spoke Korean or knew Korean culture. I did not think of myself as Korean, however, because I was raised by a non-Korean family. I felt that because of people's assumptions regarding my face, my birth made me privy to a culture I did not know. I felt like an imposter. I only knew American culture.

In college I wanted to understand the racial implications of my face. I sought to reconcile the identity nurtured by my experience with my adoptive family and the identity imposed by the racial stereotypes of my society. Despite how I had grown up, as an American, *being* American was a function of color. I felt that I did not fit in, either in the world of my birth, because I knew nothing about Korean culture, or the world in which I had grown up, because I did not look "American." I realized that the conflict in my identity arose in part because I was only given two choices: Korean or American. There was no place, except in my family, for me to be both or neither.

After college I saw that the question "who am I?" has never been answered except by a resounding declaration of who I am. Who I am is a transcultural, multicultural, interracial, hybrid, hyphenated, worlds-bridging being. I am not a "half" or a "quarter" or a "third" anything. I am one being, shaped by my experiences. I have an Asian face, an Irish last name, a blond-haired mother. As I came to accept the paradoxes and contradictions of my identity, I appreciated the richness brought to my life by my many dualities. I have two countries and two families. My Korean birth mother and father gave birth to my body; my adoptive mother and father gave birth to my soul. Because of their choices I am of two worlds, a bridge between two cultures. The East gave me life. The West taught me how to live it.

At the most profound level of our human souls is our ability to love. My adoptive parents were not and will never be perfect. It is because of their humanity that their choice to adopt was so extraordinary. Stepping beyond traditional definitions of family and transcending their childhood experiences of racism, my adoptive parents chose to love another human being. Although blood may be thicker than water, my adoption has demonstrated to me that love is thicker than blood.

The act of adoption is one moment in a person's life, but its meaning is a lifelong journey of self-discovery. I knew I was not the only person who felt she had been caught between worlds, walking on a fence between identities. Knowing that there were approximately one hundred thousand Korean-born adoptees in the United States, I sought to create an organization dedicated to sharing and celebrating the experiences of international and interracial adoptions and to establishing a community of transcultural people—individuals whose lives bridge nations, cultures, and races. The name of the organization is "also-known-as," a recognition of our self identities and human experiences not apparent on our surfaces. As we choose to embrace the contradictions that arise from our dual identities, we are given an opportunity to shatter racial and cultural stereotypes and empower others to see the dignity of the individual. In a world separated by fear, hatred, and prejudice, international and interracial families are an example of the greatness of our human spirits, which can shift mind and heart to embrace and love a stranger as a daughter or a son, a sister or a brother. I was a stranger, taken by choice into my adoptive parents' home and given a family.

Thank you, Mom and Dad, for giving me so many choices.

Magnificent Mission: Answering the Call

PEG MARENGO AND ALISON SMITH

WORCESTER, MASSACHUSETTS

OUR SIX ADULT CHILDREN were born in the mid sixties. They came, bringing a plenitude of diapers, and raced through their teens in a flurry of dance classes, karate, and music lessons. Then, suddenly, they all had jobs or were off to school. It was a perfect setup for a severe case of empty-nest syndrome.

We returned to study and work full-time, teaching music and graphic arts, setting up day care centers, and working with at-risk teens. Our rich, full lives still revolved around children, yet we longed for just one more child of our own. When Peggy was diagnosed with colon cancer, that dream seemed to be out of the question. Given her poor prognosis we chose to pursue alternative treatment instead of the traditional cancer protocols. We wanted the time that was left to be quality time with our family.

At a time when little was known about caring for HIV-infected babies and fear fueled by ignorance swept the country, Peggy Marengo and Alison Smith created a second family based on loving and consistent care. Peggy's own words say it best: "It is overwhelming to imagine that we may continue to lose our children, one by one, to their various illnesses. Yet if we hadn't had the courage to proceed twelve years ago, accepting the challenge of loss that we all must face, we would not have experienced the greatest joy of our lives, our children."

In the fall of 1985, as Peg lay recovering from surgery, we received Elizabeth Kübler-Ross's newsletter, *Death and Dying.* In it she called for a few spunky volunteers willing to parent institutionalized children suffering from AIDS. We wondered, could this be our calling? We were already confronting death and dealing with its quirks and surprises. Fostering a terminally ill child who was innocently staring down the belly of the beast seemed a reasonable answer to our empty-nest dilemma. Peggy's recovery was a work in progress; why not share our strength, parenting a child with a terminal diagnosis? With no knowledge of how social welfare systems and agencies worked, we just plunged in.

Elizabeth herself returned our call, interviewed us for a long time, and ultimately visited us. She understood how critical it is to be discriminating when recruiting caregivers for special needs and terminally ill children. Many people truly want to be of service but haven't thought through what it takes in terms of time and emotional and physical commitment. Elizabeth took us under her wing and gave us the tremendous benefit of her influence and knowledge. Her sole mission was to get Luci, one particular child who had won her heart, into a loving home. After seven months of interviews, meetings, and stress, we finally were allowed to meet Luci. By then she was nearly two years old and had lived in hospitals all of her young life. That first night, we stayed next to her crib, watching her as

she slept. Luci woke in the night, looked at us with knowing eyes, and reached out to touch us. It was love at first sight.

When Luci finally came home with us on her second birthday, she was given only six months to live. She could neither walk nor talk, and the consensus was that she never would. These were the dark ages in our understanding of the AIDS virus, when most children died within two years of diagnosis.

With the help of one of our adult sons, a professional dancer, we began an exercise regimen to build her atrophied muscles. We began the long process of weaning her off the gastric tube that fed her in the hospital by introducing baby foods with different textures to desensitize her mouth. We also began speech therapy to encourage vocalization. Today all of these therapies are taken for granted, but in 1986 they were considered a waste of time for one not expected to live long enough to benefit from them. Since she had failed to thrive on every formula her doctors had tried, we devised our own, a rich, multifaceted formula soon nicknamed "Luci's Magic Formula" by the hospital. It worked, and Luci thrived.

Although she was a toddler chronologically, Luci did not have even the most basic infant's skills in terms of development. She had never been outside of the hospital, and as a result her depth perception was impaired for years, hampering her ability to deal with stairs. These deficits of institutionalization allowed us to experience many of

Luci's firsts. We saw our two-year-old as she tried to catch a breeze with her little hand, as she listened to the rustle of leaves overhead, as she first turned her cheek to feel the air on her face, and when she put her bare feet on the grass for the first time. These are the cherished memories of mothers.

Over the years Luci nearly succumbed to her disease more than once. We watched her cope with dementia and the ravages of AIDS, always fighting and struggling back to us, with greater determination each time. In a decade of irrational fear and poor education about HIV we were blessed with a supportive neighborhood and a growing circle of loving friends. It would take years, however, for some of our own family members to realize that their fears were unfounded. All the while, Luci, the first child with AIDS placed and adopted in our state (and as far as we know, the first such adoption in the country), was making her own profound contribution to society's understanding of her disease. Her love of life—and her continuing survival—awakened people to the needs of innocent, HIV-infected children and lessened their own fears of contracting the virus.

Peg wondrously recovered as our family grew. When Luci was four years old, Ida and Lotti joined our family, then came Molly, a severely multiply challenged one-year-old with kidney cancer and cerebral palsy, supported by tubes and machines. There was a lot to do and an exciting life to live.

Next was Bea, an HIV-positive three-month-old weighing only five pounds who suffered from various cranial, facial, and neck anomalies. Then came Kessie, who like her siblings, had been exposed to drugs and alcohol in utero. A year later we welcomed Gabriel, HIV-positive and battling severe alcohol and drug withdrawal, who had been born to parents institutionalized since childhood with schizophrenia. Last to come was Wayne, whose premature birth and severe drug and alcohol exposure seriously compounded his battle with sickle-cell anemia.

As our children came to us, we had to let go of our own agendas and let them teach us what they needed to reach their potential. One principle was clear from the start, however—we were a family first. Illness and challenges were just another facet of our lives, balanced by love, activities, education, respect, and the joy of living. By choosing to be a family first, we reinforced the fact that although the child owns the illness or challenge, the entire family copes with it. Our children are never alone with pain or fear. In the hospital or at home, one of us is always there, fighting their fight with them, side by side. There is a lesson to be learned here for those that do not understand adoption, much less the special needs of these children. Ours are not just children we have "taken in." They are *our* children, and we are their family. Love and bonding do not discriminate between biological and adopted children.

Trust Your Instincts and Keep It Simple

Philip and Alice Hammerstein Mathias
Peter Mathias and Melinda Walsh
Harrison, NY

Pearl S. Buck, raised by missionary parents in China, started Welcome House in 1949 to find adoptive families for children of Asian-American parentage. Alice and Philip Mathias's daughter, Melinda, born in this country of Japanese and American parents, was the first infant placed for adoption by Ms. Buck. Peter, whose background was the same as that of his sister, was adopted three years later. My conversations with Philip, Alice, and their grown children, Peter and Melinda, revealed much about the early days of transracial adoption in this country.

PHILIP: Alice and I chose to adopt for one very simple reason. I couldn't make babies, and we wanted them. I had no problem with adoption from the very start. As far as I was concerned, these were our children and that was that.

ALICE: When Philip and I decided to adopt we really had no other choice. Phil's approach to most things was to take his time and to weigh every possibility before he made a decision, but when my stepmother asked if we'd be interested in adopting a biracial Asian-American baby, he said, "Sure!" immediately. My father, Oscar Hammerstein, was a friend of Pearl Buck. Turning to Welcome House, the foundation she started to help find homes for these children, was an obvious choice. My mother, who considered herself quite a liberal, was shocked at first. Of course, as soon as she held

Melinda she was won over immediately. Still, even my father, who was chairman of the Welcome House board, asked if we'd consider a Caucasian child when we were ready for a second. "Oh, no!" I told him, letting him know it was a silly question.

PETER: What appears complex about adoption is really so simple: less is more. My parents raised us with instinctive common sense, a respect and love of life, and strong family values.

MELINDA: I couldn't agree more. I had more support than most kids, and that had nothing to do with being adopted. My parents were always behind us. If we made a mistake, we knew they would be supportive and help us get beyond it. Everything you could want in a parent was there in mine. I never thought "adoptive parents." They were just *my* parents. But as far as adoption not being complex, I don't necessarily agree. We don't look at all like our parents, and anyone can see that there's something different here. I felt as if I went through life explaining my situation. It's not exactly uncomfortable, but it does become tedious. The funny thing was that my parents just never could see the difference. They're color blind.

ALICE: We encountered some negativity, even outright hostility, from some of our neighbors when we adopted each of our children in the early fifties. Racism, especially toward interracial unions and the children born of them, was both subtle and direct. Philip and I simply chose to ignore the hostility, because racism is an ignorant position. It's difficult to fight ignorance other than by positive example. We loved our children, tried to respond to their concerns and interests, and led normal lives.

PETER: In a sense our family was a lab test. Our experiences couldn't be discussed over coffee with another family going through the same things; there *were* virtually no other families like ours. As far as blatant racism goes, it was probably easier for me as an adolescent than it was for Melinda. I wasn't automatically aligned with any of the dominant groups in our town—Irish, Italian, or Jewish—so this uniqueness really worked for me.

MELINDA: Did I feel that I was ever the object of racism? No. I would hear racial slurs and comments that were not entirely complimentary, but more from adults than from kids I knew. These were usually made in passing, especially if the person making them wasn't aware of my background. They were uneducated comments. Someone might say, "You look a little Chinky."

ALICE: Peter and Melinda had questions about adoption that were appropriate for their ages as they grew up. I remember a valuable piece of advice that Pearl Buck gave us. She said to answer a child's question briefly and to wait until they ask. One night when Melinda was about three she asked, "Who fixed me up? Who put my arm on and my leg on and my head on, too?" That was a tough one, but I simply explained that the people who had conceived her did all that. She seemed satisfied. Peter wasn't always so eager for answers. Once as we prepared to go to visit Pearl Buck the next day, I explained to him that she was the lady who found him for us and asked if he wanted me to tell him

about it. Peter shook his head vigorously. "Oh, no," he said. "I'm not ready to learn about birth yet!" I said nothing else. Pearl's was one of the best bits of advice I'd ever received!

Children, in their innocent curiosity about everything, often asked direct questions not aimed to hurt or tease but simply to learn the answer. A child we met at the playground pointed to Melinda and asked me, "What race is she?" I didn't have to think long. "The human race," I said. On another occasion a young boy asked, "What kind of eyes has he got? Are they Chinese eyes or Jewish eyes?" "They're American eyes," I replied. "Aren't they beautiful?" The boy nodded and went on playing.

I remember when Peter, always sensitive and creative and with a great sense of fun, came to us one day when he was around eight and asked, "What am I? Japanese, or what?" I explained that he was American with a half-Japanese background. He thought for a moment and said, "Ah, so-o-o!"

PETER: Life is simple when you boil it down to the basics: friends and family. Each of us eventually becomes at peace with who he or she is, and that gives us our sense of direction. My parents did what they did out of love and the deepest desire to have a family, trusting their instincts along the way. Life is really very simple that way.

Twenty Years of Single Parenthood

KATHY ECCLES

DENVER, COLORADO

I GUESS I WAS SOMETHING OF A PIONEER, or just downright crazy, when I decided to be artificially inseminated twenty-one years ago. By my late twenties I was getting very tired of borrowing other people's children and taking them to the zoo and felt that I was really ready to be a mother. As there was no prospective husband waiting in the wings, and I didn't sleep around, I realized that I would have to do it alone. Adoption was my initial choice, as a friend of mine had adopted two children from overseas, but at that time

In 1977 Kathy Eccles became the first single woman in the Denver area to be artificially inseminated. Long before the procedure and sperm banks became common, Kathy, then twenty-nine, was inseminated by an anonymous donor from Denver General Hospital. Called everything from shameful to crazy, she received hate mail, experienced the loss of several close friendships, and even suffered temporary estrangement from her family. But she and her daughter Laura, now twenty, have a strong and powerful relationship.

most children who were available to single women had special needs. I was afraid that I wouldn't have the time or money to raise a child with a disability.

Since I worked at a medical center, many of my friends were doctors. When I mentioned my desire to be a mother an obstetrician suggested that I talk to his partner, who was performing artificial inseminations for some of his patients. I

knew nothing about the procedure and the doctor had only inseminated married women up until then, but after we talked he was more than willing to work with me. He and his partner checked with an attorney and wrote up a legal document stating that there would be no guarantees regarding either the health or the physical characteristics of the baby. At that time there were no sophisticated sperm banks like there are today, and most of the donors were poor men who donated for the twenty-five dollars they were paid for each vial of sperm. I just wanted to know that the donor and his family had a clean bill of health. The only other requirement was that he had to have fathered other children, so I would know he wasn't shooting blanks. There were no records or names of the donor, only a pager number that, when activated, alerted the doctor to send the specimen to the waiting recipient. All I know was that my specimen came from Denver General Hospital.

When word got around work that I was considering getting pregnant as a single woman, I got all sorts of weird offers of "help." Several of my male coworkers jokingly volunteered their services, and one man said he would love to be the father of my child but did not want a sexual relationship. To this day I don't understand what he meant.

I was nervous and apprehensive about whether it would really work but decided that whatever happens, happens. Each month I would go to the clinic and get inseminated, three days in a row when I was ovulating. I was on my fifth cycle, each round costing $125 twenty years ago, and had run out of money. That last month my doctor used three different donors from Denver General, and that seemed to do the trick; I was pregnant. But my doctor was the last to know. After the final insemination I had started to spot and assumed I wasn't pregnant. But since I worked in a medical lab, I had the test administered anyway. When it came back positive, I called my doctor and told him that I was pregnant.

At the same time that I became pregnant a prominent male doctor at our medical center came out of the closet, so we got a lot of media attention and became gossip central. Most of my friends were very supportive of my decision to become a single mother and buffered me against the prejudice, but I still felt disapproval from many friends and colleagues. I even got hate letters through the interoffice mail. The most absurd reaction I received was from a close friend who pulled away because she was concerned that as a single mother I wouldn't be able to afford to send my child to college. I frequently think about that conversation now that Laura is attending a private college and spending her junior year abroad.

Unfortunately, my family was not very supportive of my decision either. My mother and stepfather did not want me to get pregnant, so I literally ran away from them, staying with friends for several weeks while making the decision to try one last time to get pregnant. My mother initially thought that I had done a shameful thing and didn't tell her friends about Laura until she was seven months old. My stepfather wouldn't even look at my daughter for several months after she was born. I confronted them both and said that if they couldn't accept my child then I couldn't see them anymore. They had a really long talk and started to realize that Laura was a blessing in all our lives.

One thing that was very important to me when making the decision to get pregnant was that Laura would have a strong male role model in her life. The man I asked to be her godfather assured me that he would love her as his own, and he has. He has been very active in her life, and I never felt that I was doing this alone. When Laura was two years old she asked me where her dad was. I've always believed that knowledge is a very powerful thing, so I told her that I had really wanted a child, and as I was not married, I decided to have her in a different way.

To me, being a parent is an opportunity to share with our children everything that we have learned. My love for Laura is absolute, but I feel that she is just on loan to me to raise until she reaches womanhood. I cannot believe that she is now twenty and no longer has time to go to the zoo with me. Two decades later I am still borrowing other people's children and taking them there.

Afterword

Dave Thomas, Founder of Wendy's International

Dave Thomas was born in New Jersey to an unwed mother and adopted shortly after his birth by a Michigan couple. His experience with adoption was not all that positive. His adoptive mother died when he was five, and Dave and his father drifted around the country, looking for work and staying in trailers and modest apartments. Dave found stability in the love of a strong adoptive grandmother—Minnie Sinclair—who looked out for his welfare and helped shape his beliefs about life. Obviously, something clicked. Today Dave Thomas is an adoption advocate for special-needs children needing permanent, loving homes.

BEING ADOPTED has had a big influence on the way I've looked at life and how I came to choose adoption as my personal crusade. A few years back President George Bush challenged me to lead his special initiative on adoption as spokesman for the more than thirty thousand special-needs children who needed permanent homes. Now, some of you might raise an eyebrow if you knew that my own adopted childhood was not all that happy, but I think adoption turned out to be a big plus for me. Had I not been adopted, I might have ended up a ward of the state or been raised in a county orphanage. Having a family sure beats either of those options! There's no reason in the world that a dirt-poor kid like me, a high-school dropout from a jumbled home, should have made it in life, but I did. If you keep your eye on the main things, the plain things, and do them well, you can have the success you desire.

It's a fact that all children deserve a loving family. But it doesn't always work out that way. There are thousands of children of all ages that lack a family they can call theirs, and they're looking for help. Even if it's a long and bumpy journey, adoption can be a pretty decent solution to a heartbreaking problem. There are five reasons why adoption means enough to me to make it my personal crusade:

1. There are kids in this country who are growing up in makeshift orphanages or shelters in converted office space and even worse. That's a public disgrace in the most powerful country in the world.
2. Without a home, guidance, and affection, the chances of a child's making it in this world are mighty slim.
3. Children raised without homes and families often end up in trouble and become burdens to society.
4. If you have had the blessing of a good home life yourself, you owe something back.
5. The world works on families; it really does. Fear of the unknown shouldn't stop you from being an adoptive parent.

"But . . . special needs?" you ask. Every child is special, and every child has needs. "Special needs" is only the buzz phrase that replaced "hard to place" in describing many of the children available today for adoption. The greatest need—the common denominator that identifies these children more than race, age, handicap, or disability—is their urgent need for a family. Now, I know that there are still some people who get hung up on the idea that adopted children should *blend in* with their parents, even look pretty much like them, if that can be arranged. But kids are what they are—all shapes, ages, abilities, sizes, and races. The idea behind adoption is to give kids the stability that only love and a home can provide, not to coordinate their hair and eyes with those of a prospective adoptive parent, as if matching them up will make "the *A* word" go away.

Honesty can't survive where secrecy also resides. When families keep secrets about adoption, for any reason, it ends up hurting everyone sooner or later.

International adoption has changed the old "look-alike" attitude somewhat, because the children rarely resemble their adoptive parents. But when these same families don't take advantage of the abundant support that's out there for them, they're probably hiding from the truth and pretending that their child's adoption was nothing more than a one-time event. Adoption needs to be understood as a healthy choice and a lifelong process. Families who don't grasp this miss out on a wonderful opportunity to learn and to give back to others in the name of adoption. Successful people—and successful adoptive families—have an obligation to use their personal success to draw attention to adoption as a worthwhile cause. One of the best advertisements for adoption today is a good example—*your* family.

Useful Family-Building Resources

ADOPTION RESOURCES

THE NATIONAL ADOPTION INFORMATION CLEARINGHOUSE (NAIC) 10530 Rosehaven St., Ste. 400, Fairfax VA 22030, makes referrals to additional sources and offers free fact sheets on various adoption-related topics.

THE AMERICAN ACADEMY OF ADOPTION ATTORNEYS P.O. Box 3305, Washington DC, publishes a booklet for those interested in independent adoption and lists members in each state who specialize in adoption.

INTERNATIONAL CONCERNS FOR CHILDREN 911 Cypress Dr., Boulder CO 80303, is a photo-listing service featuring photos and descriptions of over five hundred children from around the world. Donation is $25 for a twelve-month subscription, updated monthly.

THE NORTH AMERICAN COUNCIL ON ADOPTABLE CHILDREN 970 Raymond Ave., Ste. 106, St. Paul MN 55114, is a professional organization concerned with domestic adoption, especially of waiting children.

ROOTS & WINGS ADOPTION MAGAZINE P.O. Box 577, Hackettstown NJ 07840, or e-mail: adoption@interactive.net or www.adopting.org/rw.html, is a national quarterly publication containing both first-person accounts of families' adoption experiences as well as informative articles by professionals. $19.95 per year, only by subscription.

ADOPTIVE FAMILIES OF AMERICA 2309 Como Ave., St. Paul MN 55108, is a national nonprofit group that makes referrals to local adoptive parent support groups and provides an excellent eighty-page information guide ($4.95) that will interest those new to adoption, both domestic and international. They also publish a bimonthly magazine called **Adoptive Families** for $24.95 per year.

TAPESTRY BOOKS, publisher of **The Adoption Book Catalog,** (800) 765-2367 or http://www.tapestrybooks.com, is the largest source for up-to-date adoption and infertility literature. Call for a free catalog or suggestions to meet your needs or interests.

PERSPECTIVES PRESS, (317) 872-3055 or http://www.perspectivespress.com, and its publisher-author-lecturer Pat Johnston have been providing everything that's anything related to reproductive health education, adoption information and education, and related topics, since 1982.

THE HANDBOOK FOR SINGLE ADOPTIVE PARENTS (6TH EDITION), is available for $20 from the National Council for Single Adoptive Parents, P.O. Box 15084, Chevy Chase MD 20825.

THE ADOPTION RESOURCE EXCHANGE FOR SINGLE PARENTS, INC. (ARESP) P.O. Box 5782, Springfield VA 22150, e-mail: aresp@aol.com, is a single-parent advocacy group, headed by Elmy Martinez, that publishes a bimonthly newsletter, available by contacting them.

ADOPTION TODAY: Options & Outcomes, by Cynthia Peck, is an informative ninety-six page resource and story guide for prospective adoptive parents who want to know: *What are my choices? How long will the process take? What about the health of the children available? What costs can I anticipate?* $15.95 to P.O. Box 577, Hackettstown NJ 07840

INFERTILITY RESOURCES

THE ORGANIZATION OF PARENTS THROUGH SURROGACY P.O. Box 213, Wheeling IL 60090, (847) 394-4116, e-mail OPTS@starnetine.com, which is not affiliated with any surrogacy practitioner, agency, or lawyer, publishes an annual newsletter, holds regional meetings, and has an extensive telephone support network.

RESOLVE, INC. 1310 Broadway, Somerville MA 02144-1731, (617) 623-1156 is a national nonprofit organization that has assisted people in resolving their infertility by providing information, support, and advocacy. Members receive the quarterly national newsletter and a newsletter from their local chapter with news of symposia, focus workshops, and preadopt meetings.

THE INTERNATIONAL COUNCIL ON INFERTILITY INFORMATION DISSEMINATION, INC. (INCIID) P.O. Box 6836, Arlington VA 22206, email: INCIIDinfor@inciid.org, is a nonprofit organization devoted to helping couples experiencing infertility. They provide fact sheets; referrals to professional services and nonprofits; news about medication, technology, and treatment; and announcements of conferences and seminars of interest. They have comprehensive links to over 150 additional resources.

GIFTS (GUIDANCE, INFORMATION, FRIENDSHIP THROUGH SURROGACY) 1697 Market St., Santa Clara CA 95050, 1-800-444-2015, is an informational group for women who are surrogates or would like to become surrogates.

INTERNET RESOURCES: ADOPTION AND INFERTILITY

http://adoption.com is a rapidly growing commercial site that offers visitors a comprehensive array of informative sites, articles, chat rooms, and links to every aspect of adoption. A good place to start.

http://www.adoptiononline.com brings together prospective adoptive parents and pregnant women making adoption plans for their child.

http://www.iwe.com/apact.html is the site for PACT, An Adoption Alliance, which helps African-American, Latino, Asian, and multiracial children in the United States find permanent adoptive homes. Founders Beth Hall and Gail Steinberg are strong educators in the area of multicultural adoption and family dynamics. They publish an excellent agency quarterly for $24 annually and keep a comprehensive multicultural bookstore.

http://www.inet.net/adopt/html is the Internet address for **Faces of Adoption,** the AdoptionQuest Home Page that features profiles of waiting children across the country.

http://www.adopting.org is an easy-to-use site with an incredible amount of useful information for all triad members. Prospective parents will find thoughtful articles on any aspect of getting started, as well as links to agencies, lawyers, and referral resources, organized by state.

http://www.rainbowkids.com is the home of Rainbow Kids, an online magazine that deals primarily with international adoption.

http://www.opts.com is the site for the Organization of Parents Through Surrogacy (OPTS), which functions as a community resource and is dedicated to providing information, education, networking, support, and referrals to those interested in pursuing this choice.

http://www.surrogacy.com is the site for the American Surrogacy Center, Inc., and is the most complete source of surrogacy and egg donation information on the Web. Surrogacy is a growing family-building option and alternative to adoption for couples experiencing infertility. The site provides legal, medical, psychological, personal, agency, and surrogacy directories, message boards, classified advertising, e-mail discussion groups, and on-line support groups.